RISE INSPIRED:
REAL TALK. REAL FAITH. REAL LIFE.

Calvin Allen

PROLOGUE

Welcome.

I do not know where you are as you open these pages. You are standing on the mountaintop, celebrating victories. Or you are in the valley, wondering if tomorrow will be brighter. Wherever you find yourself today, I want you to know this: You are not alone.

Rise Inspired was born out of real moments both the highs that made me shout for joy and the lows that taught me to whisper prayers through tears. This book is not about perfection or having it all figured out. It is about showing up every day with an open heart, ready to receive grace and give gratitude.

I believe in the power of words. Words can break or build, heal or hurt, bind us in fear, or set us free in faith. My hope is that the words on these pages speak life into your soul, strengthen your spirit, and remind you of who you are and Whose you are.

This is not just a book to read. It is a journey to walk. A daily invitation to rise inspired, grounded, and full of faith.

So, take a deep breath. Let go of yesterday's worries. Step into today with hope. Let us rise together.

Welcome to *Rise Inspired: Real Talk. Real Faith. Real Life.*

IN DEDICATION

To every soul who has ever felt weary but chose to rise again.

To those who believe, even when it is hard.

To my family, my friends, and every person who has poured love and light into my life — thank you for helping me become who I am today.

And to God, the ultimate author of my story. May every word bring Him glory.

TABLE OF CONTENTS

 INTRODUCTION

Start your day with gratitude, faith, and encouragement. *Rise Inspired: Real Talk. Real Faith. Real Life.*is your daily dose of hope and strength, designed to uplift your spirit and remind you that you are not alone God's love and grace are with you always.

✦ PART ONE: Start with God

"May you never forget on your best day that you still need God as desperately as you did on your worst day."

"In all things pray but remember to be grateful and always give thanks."

"Be Anxious for Nothing and remember whatever you're going through that God got you."

"Cast all of your cares and anxiety on God and remember that he cares for you!! Nothing is impossible for him!!"

📌 *Reflection Prompt:*
Take 3 deep breaths. What is one thing you can surrender to God today?

🏔 PART TWO: Faith Over Fear

"Let your faith be bigger than your fear!!"

"You can do all things through Christ that strengthens you."

"God is not delaying but preparing you for everything you've prayed for."

"Faith in God includes faith in His timing. Remember, do not ever lose your faith in God!!"

📝 *Mini Affirmation:*

"I trust in God's plan even when I don't understand it."

❦ PART THREE: Grow Through What You Go Through

"Grow through what you go through!!"

"Life will test you, not to show your weaknesses, but to reveal your strengths."

"Sometimes in life, you've got to be your own coach, your own cheerleader, and your own fan."

"God sometimes takes us into troubled waters—not to drown us but to teach us."

✹ *Encouragement Corner:*

Your struggle is your strength in disguise. Keep going.

❤️ PART FOUR: Love, Worth, and Boundaries

"Love yourself. Know your worth. Accept growth. Appreciate life."

"Be brave enough to choose yourself even when others don't."

"Love yourself first, because that's who you'll be spending the rest of your life with."

"You teach people how to treat you by deciding what you will and won't accept!!"

📌 *Reminder:*

You do not have to set yourself on fire to keep others warm.

✸ PART FIVE: Live Bold. Dream Big. Do not Quit.

"You woke up today, you're breathing, you're talking, you're thinking… so that means you're Blessed!!"

"Set goals. Push yourself. Move. Do not quit. No excuses. Be awesome."

"What is meant for you will come to you in this life."

"Work hard. Dream big. Never give up!!"

📖 *Morning Declaration:*

"I was born to win. Today, I choose to walk in purpose."

 PART SIX: Stay Encouraged, Stay Covered

"May God continue to keep you, and your family covered today."

"I'm literally praying for you today that God will meet every one of your needs!! All is Well."

"To that one soul reading this I know you're tired but keep fighting."

"Your name is being spoken in rooms your feet haven't even entered yet!!"

Closing Prayer:

God, cover me today with your peace and strength. I trust you to guide my steps.

Welcome to "Rise Inspired: Real Talk. Real Faith. Real Life." — a collection of hope, faith, and encouragement to start your day with a smile and a grateful heart.

Life is full of difficulties. Some mornings we wake up feeling joyful and ready to conquer the day, and other days it feels like the weight of the world is on our shoulders. But no matter what kind of day you are facing, I want you to remember one thing: you are never alone.

I created this book as a reminder from my heart to yours that faith and gratitude have the power to change everything. Over the years, I have learned that beginning each morning with a positive thought, a prayer, or simply a moment of reflection can set the tone for an entire day of peace and purpose.

Whether you are walking through a season of challenge or celebrating a season of joy, these quotes and reflections are here to lift you up. They are not just words on a page; they are pieces of wisdom I have gathered from my own journey, inspired by faith, and tested through life's highs and lows.

This book is your companion for quiet mornings, busy days, or restless nights. Each page is an invitation to pause, breathe, and connect with something bigger than yourself.

I hope these quotes bring you comfort, courage, and a renewed sense of hope. May you find strength in these pages, just like I have.

Thank you for letting me be a part of your mornings. Let us start this journey together — one happy morning at a time.

With gratitude,
Calvin Allen

About Calvin Allen

Calvin Allen is a visionary entrepreneur, motivational mentor, and community leader from Mount Pleasant, South Carolina. A proud graduate of Wando High School and a current student at Charleston Southern University, Calvin is pursuing his bachelor's degree in professional studies while continuing to impact lives across the globe.

As the CEO and Founder of Nfinity International, LLC a premier photography firm with clients in cities such as Charlotte, Houston, Montego Bay, Atlanta, and New York. Calvin Allen has spent over two decades helping people rediscover their confidence, self-worth, and purpose through the lens of his camera. His work in photography is rooted in a deep desire to empower others and elevate their voices and stories.

Calvin Allen's commitment to service extends far beyond business. He is actively involved in outreach work feeding the homeless, visiting the sick in hospitals, and mentoring at-risk boys and girls. His mission is to help young people make a complete turnaround in life and begin choosing better paths. Through programs like Be a Mentor, Boyz to Men Mentoring Program, and Palmetto Hope Network, as well as his work on the boards of Positive Vibes Ronjanae Smith, Inc., the Jeremiah Henry Kendrick Foundation, and Black Wall Street Business Group, Calvin continues to plant seeds of change in his community.

Each morning, Calvin shares an inspiring quote via social media and text not just to fuel his own journey, but to lift others. His belief in the power of words and consistency led him to author this book. His goal is simple yet profound: to inspire hearts, renew minds, and spark positive transformation around the world.

This book reflects that mission and a reminder that no matter where you start, it is never too late to rewrite your story. Like many of you, I have faced my share of struggles, doubts, and moments were giving up seemed like the easiest choice. But through it all, I have discovered the incredible power of faith, gratitude, and choosing to speak life over my circumstances.

I have also learned, the prayers I have prayed, and the encouragement I have received along the way. My hope is that by sharing these words with you, you will find a source of daily inspiration to help you navigate your own path.

Every new day is a gift, a fresh start, and an opportunity to embrace hope and possibility. And sometimes, all we need is a little reminder a simple phrase or thought to change the direction of our day.

I do not have all the answers, but I know that leaning on God and choosing to see the good has made all the difference in my life. And that is why I want to share this with you.

You are not alone. You are stronger than you realize. And no matter what, better days are coming.

Thank you for joining me on this journey. Let us keep moving forward together, one happy morning at a time.

— Calvin Allen

CHAPTER 1

STARTING EACH DAY WITH FAITH

"May you never forget on your best day that you still need God as desperately as you did on your worst day."

We all have those days when everything feels like it is going right — the sun is shining, your goals are moving forward, and life seems smooth. On those days, it is easy to forget just how much we rely on something greater than ourselves. But here is the truth: faith is not just for the tough times. It is for every moment in between.

I remember a time when things were going great for me — work was flowing, relationships felt strong, and I was on top of the world. And yet, I felt this quiet whisper inside, reminding me to stay humble, to stay connected to my faith. Because when things change — and they will — that connection is what will carry me through.

Faith is like the foundation of a house. You do not notice it much when everything is steady, but if the storms come, it is what keeps you standing. That foundation is what gives us strength, hope, and peace that does not depend on our circumstances.

So how do we keep that foundation strong? It starts with daily habits — a quiet moment of prayer, a thankful heart, or just pausing to remember that we are not alone. Even when life feels great, choosing to acknowledge God's presence keeps us grounded.

This chapter is an invitation: Start your day with faith. Not because you are weak or struggling, but because you are wise enough to know that no matter what happens, you have a source of strength that never fails.

One simple practice that has helped me start every day with faith is writing down three things I am thankful for each morning. It might sound small or even a little basic, but I promise you, focusing on gratitude has the power to change everything. When you take a moment to pause and reflect on what is already good in your life, it shifts your whole mindset. Instead of diving into the day feeling overwhelmed or anxious, you begin with a heart full of thanks. That is when faith really starts to take root — because gratitude reminds us of who has been with us all along, through the highs and the lows.

Speaking affirmations is another powerful tool that I've leaned on. Simple declarations like, *"God is with me today,"* or *"I am strong because of His love,"* help me stay grounded when doubt or fear tries to creep in. Words matter, more than we often realize. When we speak truth to ourselves, it shapes the way we think and feel. And when our thoughts are rooted in faith, it's easier to face challenges with confidence and hope.

Let me share a little bit about my own journey. There was a time when I faced some big uncertainties — a new job, moving to a different city, and family situations that left me feeling uncertain about the future. Some days, the worry felt so heavy I wasn't sure how I would get through. But each morning, no matter how I felt, I made it a habit to pray, even if it was just a few quiet moments. That simple daily connection with God didn't just bring me peace; it gave me the strength and courage I needed to keep going. Faith became my anchor in the storm.

Here is what I want you to know: you do not have to have it all figured out. Faith is not about having every answer. It grows slowly, when you choose it again, especially in the small, ordinary moments. When you wake up and decide to trust that things will work out, even if you do not see how yet, that's faith. And that is powerful.

CHAPTER 2

EMBRACING JOY IN EVERYDAY MOMENTS

Life is not always about big wins or grand celebrations. Sometimes, joy shows up quietly—in the trivial things we might overlook if we are rushing through the day. The sound of birds singing outside your window, a warm cup of coffee in the morning, or a genuine smile from a stranger can all remind us that happiness is often found in simple moments.

I have learned that embracing joy does not mean ignoring life's challenges or pretending everything is perfect. Instead, it is about choosing to notice the good, even when things feel hard. It is about training our hearts to see light in the shadows.

One of my favorite reminders is this: **"May you never forget on your best day that you still need God as desperately as you did on your worst day. Never forget that."** This quote keeps me grounded, reminding me that no matter how high we rise, we still need faith and gratitude to carry us through.

Start with Gratitude

Gratitude is the foundation of joy. It is easy to get caught up in what is missing or what is wrong, but when you make a habit of giving thanks for what you have, even the trivial things, your perspective begins to shift. It might feel simple but trust me—it is powerful.

Try this: each morning, before you get out of bed, think of three things you are grateful for. It is the roof over your head, the people who love you, or just the fact that you woke up to a new day. This small practice sets the tone for a day filled with appreciation and joy.

As I always say, **"In all things pray but remember to be grateful and always give thanks."** When we approach life with gratitude, we invite more happiness in.

Find Joy in the Ordinary

Joy does not always announce itself with fireworks. Sometimes it is found in a child's laughter, the smell of fresh rain, or the first sip of your favorite drink. When you slow down and pay attention, you will start noticing these moments more often. Remember, you do not have to wait for a big event or milestone to feel joy. Joy is accessible right now—in this moment. It is in the way the sun feels on your face or the way a kind word from a friend lifts your spirit.

One thing I always remind myself is: **"Be Anxious for Nothing and remember whatever you're going through that God got you."** Joy can exist even in struggle when you hold onto that truth.

Laugh More

Laughter truly is medicine for the soul. When you laugh, your body releases feel-good chemicals called endorphins that reduce stress and boost your mood. Do not take life too seriously all the time—find reasons to smile and laugh every day. Whether it is watching a funny video, sharing jokes with friends, or simply finding humor in life's little quirks, laughter makes joystick around longer.

And remember, **"Treat people good, do good by people and good will come to you."** Sometimes joy comes from spreading it around.

Surround Yourself with Positivity

The people and things you surround yourself with influence your mindset. Choose to spend time with those who uplift you, encourage your dreams, and remind you of your worth. Fill your environment with things that inspire and motivate you—a favorite song, uplifting books, or inspiring quotes like these.

As the saying goes, "You become who you hang out with," so be intentional about the company you keep.

Carrying Joy with You

As you go through your days, remember that joy is not just a fleeting feeling—it is a mindset you can nurture. Life will bring difficulties, but when you intentionally look for moments of happiness and gratitude, you build resilience. Joy becomes a shield that protects your heart against life's storms.

One powerful way to keep joy close is to practice kindness—both to yourself and others. When you choose kindness, you create a ripple effect. A small act of compassion can brighten someone's day and fill your own heart with warmth. Never underestimate the power of a smile, a kind word, or simply being present for someone.

Also, do not forget to give yourself grace. Sometimes, life gets overwhelming, and it is okay to feel tired, sad, or frustrated. Joy does not mean being happy every single moment. It means knowing that even on the tough days, better moments are coming, and that you have the strength to face whatever comes your way.

I want to leave you with this reminder: **"I don't care what anyone says, happiness is a choice—and so is joy."** You can choose to focus on what lifts you up and let go of what weighs you down.

So, go ahead—embrace the little joys, hold onto your faith, and walk through each day knowing that you can find light, even in the darkest places. The journey to joy is ongoing, but it is one worth taking every day.

CHAPTER 3

FINDING STRENGTH IN FAITH AND HOPE

Life can sometimes feel heavy, like the weight of the world is pressing down on your shoulders. During those moments, faith and hope become more than just words—they become lifelines. They remind us that no matter how hard things get, there is always a reason to keep going.

Faith is not about religion or spiritual beliefs (though it can be); it is about trusting that things will work out, that you are not alone, and that there is a bigger plan at work—even when you cannot see it yet. It is the quiet voice inside that says, *"Keep going, you've got this."*

Hope is the light in the darkness. It is what keeps us dreaming, even when reality feels tough. Hope gives us a future to look forward to and the courage to face today's challenges.

Here are some thoughts to carry with you:

"Faith is taking the first step even when you don't see the whole staircase." — Martin Luther King Jr.

"Hope is the thing with feathers that perches in the soul—and sings the tunes without the words—and never stops at all." — Emily Dickinson

Remember, faith and hope do not mean that problems disappear. They mean you have the strength inside to rise above them.

More Words to Inspire Your Journey

Sometimes, it helps to hear the wisdom of others who have walked through dark valleys and found their way to the light. Here are a few more quotes to lift your spirit:

"When you come to the end of your rope, tie a knot and hold on." — Franklin D. Roosevelt

"Faith does not make things easy; it makes them possible." — Luke 1:37

"Hope is being able to see that there is light despite all of the darkness." — Desmond Tutu

"God gives the nuts, but He does not crack them." — German Proverb

Each of these reminds us that faith and hope do not mean life will not be hard. Instead, they are the tools that help us keep moving forward, even when the path looks uncertain.

Practical Tips to Build Faith and Hope Daily

Building faith and hope is not a one-time event. It is a daily practice—a choice to see beyond today's struggles and believe in a better tomorrow. Here are some simple ways to cultivate these powerful qualities:

1. Start Your Day with Gratitude

Before you jump into your daily tasks, take a moment to think about three things you are thankful for. It can be something as small as a warm cup of coffee or as big as the love of family. Gratitude opens your heart and prepares your mind to welcome faith and hope.

2. Read or Listen to Inspirational Content

Find a verse, quote, or story that resonates with you. It could be a passage from a spiritual text, a motivational book, or even a podcast that inspires you. Make it a habit to engage with uplifting content each day.

3. Practice Mindful Prayer or Meditation

Whether you pray, meditate, or simply sit quietly reflecting on your blessings and challenges, these moments of calm can deepen your faith and renew your hope. Focus on your breath, your intentions, or simply be present.

4. Surround Yourself with Positive People

Faith and hope grow stronger when shared. Spend time with people who uplift you, encourage you, and remind you of the good in life. Avoid negativity where possible—it can drain your spirit.

5. Keep a Faith and Hope Journal

Write down moments when you felt faith or hope shining through, even in tough times. Record prayers answered, signs of progress, or simply your feelings and reflections. Over time, this journal will be a treasure trove of encouragement.

6. Take Small Steps Forward

Faith and hope often require action. Set small goals each day that move you closer to your dreams. Celebrate even the tiniest victories—they are proof that progress is possible.

CHAPTER 4

SPEAK LIFE DAILY

Every morning is a clean slate—a brand-new opportunity to decide how you will show up in the world. And one of the most powerful things you can do to set the tone for your day is to *speak life*. Before the texts, the meetings, the traffic, and the responsibilities hit you—take a moment to speak something over yourself that aligns with your faith, your vision, and your purpose.

Your words are seeds, and the heart is the soil. Whatever you plant will grow.

When you speak life, you are not ignoring reality—you are declaring your trust in something greater than what you see. You are speaking from a place of faith, knowing that God moves in response to both belief and confession.

There's power in waking up and saying, *"Today is a gift, and I will live it fully."* Or *"No matter what comes, I know God has already gone before me."* Speaking life does not mean you will not face challenges—it means you are choosing to face them with courage, knowing that you are not alone.

Even when the day starts off rough, you still have a say in how it ends. You can reset your mind by resetting your mouth. You can shift the atmosphere in your home, workplace, or school simply by being the one who speaks peace, hope, and love.

When fear whispers, *"It won't work out,"* respond with, *"I believe God is working all things together for my good."* When discouragement says, *"You'll never get through this,"* say boldly, *"God has already brought me through too much to leave me now."*

Speak to your storm. Speak to your goals. Speak to your inner critic. And most importantly, speak life over yourself and those around you.

⚱ Daily Declarations to Speak

- "I am chosen. I am loved. I am equipped. I am enough."
- "My situation may look uncertain, but my faith is solid."
- "I speak peace over my life. I speak calm over my mind. I speak clarity into my decisions."
- "Every delay is working in my favor. What is meant for me is on the way."
- "I am walking in purpose, even when the path isn't clear."

More Quotes to Speak Life Daily

- "The tongue has no bones, but it is strong enough to build or break. Use it to build your future."
- "You are speaking into your tomorrow every time you open your mouth. Speak what you want to see."
- "Let your words reflect where you're going, not just where you've been."
- "Even in silence, your faith speaks loudly. Keep believing, keep speaking, and keep going."
- "God honors a heart that speaks life—especially when life feels hard."
- "Stop rehearsing your pain and start declaring your healing."
- "You were created in God's image—don't speak less over yourself than He would."
- "Do not let your circumstances mute your mouth. Speak life, no matter what it looks like."
- "Speak kindness to yourself. Your spirit is listening."
- "Your future is waiting on your words. What are you saying today?"

CHAPTER 5

GRATEFUL ON PURPOSE

Gratitude is a choice, not just a feeling. Some mornings we wake up feeling energized, and it is easy to say, "Thank you, God." But other mornings? It takes effort. That is where *grateful on purpose* comes in. It means choosing to see the beauty, the blessings, and the breakthroughs—no matter what life looks like now. Being grateful is about deciding in your heart to focus on what is right instead of what is wrong, what you have instead of what you lack.

So many times, we wait for the perfect situation before we give thanks. We say, "I'll be grateful when things get better, when the bills are paid, when the pain is gone." But what if your gratitude is the very thing that *opens the door* for those better days? What if the simple act of thanking God for what you do have shifts your entire perspective—and creates space for miracles to move in?

You may not be where you want to be, but you are not where you used to be. That alone is a testimony. Today, the only thing going right is the fact that you woke up. That is still a reason to say, "Thank you, Lord." Gratitude reminds us that we are already blessed, even if everything is not perfect. It keeps our hearts tender, our minds peaceful, and our spirits aligned with God's grace.

The more we practice gratitude, the more we start to notice the trivial things—the unexpected smile from a stranger, the sunlight breaking through the clouds, the quiet peace in the middle of a storm. Gratitude changes us from the inside out. It does not mean you ignore your pain or pretend things are perfect. It means you choose to see God's hand even when life feels uncertain.

Make it a daily habit to say, "thank you." Write it down in a journal, speak it aloud, whisper it in prayer. Thank God for your health, for your family, for the lessons in the struggle. Gratitude is your personal key to joy, and joy is your strength.

So today, no matter what is going on, be grateful on purpose. Let your heart stay lifted. Keep your spirit soft. Give God thanks for what He has already done—and watch what He will do next.

☀ Daily Grateful Thoughts

- "Thank you, God, for the gift of another day."
- "I may not have everything I want, but I have everything I need today."
- "I'm grateful for strength I didn't know I had."
- "I choose to see blessings, not burdens."
- "Even in the waiting, I'm thankful."

Quotes on Gratitude to Live By

- **"A grateful heart attracts peace. A thankful mind attracts miracles."**
- **"Gratitude turns what we have into more than enough."**
- **"When you're thankful for what God's done, He'll keep doing more."**
- **"Worry fades when gratitude grows."**
- **"Your next blessing may just be waiting on your next 'thank you.'"**
- **"The secret to joy isn't more stuff—it's more gratitude."**
- **"Say 'thank you' even when it is tough. That is faith in action."**
- **"Start and end your day with gratitude—it's the best bookend to peace."**
- **"Gratitude is your daily reminder that God is still good, still faithful, and still with you."**

CHAPTER 6

RESILIENCE AND INNER STRENGTH

Some days will stretch you. Others will try to break you. And then there are those days that feel like a full-on storm. But here is what you must remember: if God brought you to it, He would bring you through it. That quiet fire deep inside of you—that's resilience. That is the Holy Spirit whispering, "You can keep going."

Resilience does not mean you are never tired or discouraged. It means you keep walking with faith even when you are unsure of the road. You trust that God is working behind the scenes, even when it seems like nothing is changing in front of you.

Every tear you have cried, every time you chose prayer over panic, every time you smiled through your pain—that is proof you are stronger than you think. You do not need to have all the answers. You just need to trust the One who does.

Let these words pour strength into your heart:

"God didn't create you to break—He created you to rise."

"You may be tired, but you are not finished. Rest in God, then rise again."

"Do not give up. The enemy knows your breakthrough is near."

"Even if the mountain doesn't move, God will give you the strength to climb it."

"You are not what you have been through. You are who God says you are—strong, chosen, equipped, and loved."

"Some of your greatest growth will come in your hardest seasons. Keep pushing."

"Faith doesn't remove the storm; it gives you the strength to stand in it."

"You have survived 100% of your worst days. That is resilience."

"You may want to give up but remember who you belong to. Gods not finished with you yet."

"Healing takes time. Strength takes faith. Progress takes courage."

"Let your scars remind you that God heals, restores, and uses brokenness for His glory."

"You are a living testimony that God gives beauty for ashes."

"They counted you out—but God is counting you in."

"You did not come this far to quit. Keep praying, keep trusting, keep moving."

"When you're down to nothing, God is up to something."

Scripture reminders to carry you:

- *"But they that wait upon the Lord shall renew their strength; they shall mount up with wings as eagles…"*—Isaiah 40:31
- *"My grace is sufficient for you, for my power is made perfect in weakness."* —2 Corinthians 12:9
- *"The righteous may fall seven times, but they rise again."*—Proverbs 24:16
- *"Be strong and courageous. Do not be afraid… for the Lord your God goes with you."*—Deuteronomy 31:6

Resilience is not a destination—it is a daily choice. It is waking up and saying, "God, I trust You even when I don't understand You." It is holding your peace when everything around you say panic. It is knowing that your strength comes not from the world, but from the One who created the world.

So, breathe. Pray. Rise. Walk boldly into today knowing that resilience lives in your spirit and victory lives in your future.

Start your mornings with declarations of faith, hope, and love. Speak peace into your day. Proclaim that you are healed, whole, and favored by God. Do not allow doubt or fear to guide your tongue—choose to walk in boldness and victory, trusting that God is promises over your life still stand.

Morning Quotes:

🕊 *"Speak life over your situation, even if you do not see it yet. Your words are seeds. Keep planting."*

🕊 *"Declare it before you see it. Thank God for it before it arrives. Faith is believing it is already yours."*

🕊 *"You are covered by God. You are protected by God. And you are chosen by God. Walk boldly in that truth."*

🕊 *"Even when things seem quiet, trust that God is still moving behind the scenes."*

🕊 *"Do not just survive today—command the day. Let your words set the tone for peace, favor, and strength."*

🕊 *"Faith-filled words attract faith-filled outcomes. Be mindful of what you are speaking over your life."*

🕊 *"You have come too far to let fear silence your purpose. Speak with courage. Live with intention."*

Reflection

Have you ever noticed how different your day feels when you speak positively first thing in the morning? When you affirm who you are in Christ, when you encourage yourself before the world has a chance to discourage you? That is not coincidence—that's power. Your words matter. What are you declaring over your life today? Are you building up or tearing down? Let today be the day you commit to speaking life—no matter what.

Morning Prayer

Heavenly Father,

Thank You for the power of life You placed in my tongue. Help me to use my words to build up, to encourage, and to heal. Guard my mouth from negativity, fear, or doubt, and remind me to speak Your promises daily. I declare peace, favor, strength, and victory over this day. Thank You for being my source and my guide.
In Jesus' name, Amen.

Journal Prompt 📝

- What are five things you want to declare over your life this week?
- Write down three things you are believing God for. Now speak to them aloud.
- What are some phrases or thoughts you need to stop saying to yourself?

CHAPTER 7

KEEP THE FAITH, EVEN WHEN IT IS HARD

Faith is not always easy. Sometimes, it feels like you are trusting God in the dark hoping for something you cannot see and believing for something that has not arrived. But real faith grows strong in those exact moments. It is when the way is unclear that faith becomes your compass. Even when life shakes you, you must stand firm in what you know: God is faithful, God is good, and God is with you.

You do not have to have it all figured out—just believe. Your miracle is in motion, and your breakthrough is closer than you think.

Morning Quotes:

✸ *"Faith is trusting God when it does not make sense—when the 'how' and the 'when' are still unknown."*

✸ *"You may not feel strong right now, but you are still standing. That is faith in action."*

✸ *"Even on the days when you feel weary, your faith is working. Do not give up."*

✸ *"God did not bring you this far to leave you. He is still writing your story."*

✸ *"Walk by faith, not by fear. God's record of accomplishment is perfect, and He has not failed you yet."*

✸ *"The most powerful move you can make today is to keep believing."*

Reflection

Some mornings, faith feels like a whisper. Other days, it is a shout. Either way, it counts. Faith is not about always feeling strong—it is about deciding to trust even when your heart is tired. Remember that you do not have to have mountain-sized faith. Jesus said faith the size of a mustard seed can move mountains. So, start small, stay faithful, and trust big. He sees your effort. He hears your prayers. Keep walking.

Morning Prayer
Lord,

I admit that some days are harder than others. But I still believe. I still trust You. Help me to walk by faith, especially when I cannot see the outcome. Strengthen my heart, renew my spirit, and remind me that You are in control. Thank You for being faithful even when I waver. I will keep holding on to Your promises. **In Jesus' name, Amen.**

Journal Prompt

- What area of your life is requiring the most faith right now?
- Write a short letter to God sharing your fears and asking for strength.
- Describe a past situation where God came through for you, even when it looked impossible.

CHAPTER 8

EMBRACE THE UNEXPECTED

We all love a good plan. We map out our goals, create to-do lists, and imagine how life will unfold. Planning gives us comfort and a sense of control. But if there is one thing life consistently teaches us, it is that change is inevitable.

Sometimes, the change is small- a last-minute schedule shift or a minor setback. Other times, it feels like an earthquake beneath our feet — a job loss, an unexpected diagnosis, a relationship ending, or a sudden move. These moments can shake our confidence and leave us wondering where God is in the chaos.

But what if the unexpected isn't something to fear? What if it is a doorway into a deeper relationship with God? What if these surprises are invitations to trust Him more fully and to grow in ways we never imagined possible?

I have learned that some of my greatest blessings have come from doors I never meant to open and paths I never intended to walk. When I look back, I see God's fingerprints in every unexpected twist. I see His provision, His faithfulness, and His love woven through every detour.

In this chapter, I invite you to open your heart to life's surprises. Release your tight grip on the way things "should" be and trust that God's plan for your life is bigger and more beautiful than anything you could design on your own. Remember: you are not alone on this journey. Every unexpected moment is held in His loving hands.

✦ Quote

"We must be willing to let go of the life we planned so as to have the life that is waiting for us."
— Joseph Campbell

💬 Reflection

We spend so much time trying to control life's details — where we will work, who we will love, how we will achieve our dreams. We hold on so tightly because we believe that if we can just make everything go according to plan, we will finally feel safe and fulfilled.

But life does not always follow our carefully crafted blueprints. A job you thought you would have forever suddenly ends. A dream you nurtured for years does not unfold as you hoped. Or life calls you to move away from everything familiar.

These moments of surprise can feel like a storm tearing through your soul. Yet, in the middle of that storm, there is often an invitation to grow closer to God. In my own life, when plans fell apart, I discovered a deeper faith and strength I never knew I had.

God sees the full picture. He knows the connections, the people, and the opportunities waiting for you just beyond that closed door. When you surrender your expectations, you make room for His divine creativity to shape your journey.

Instead of clinging to "what should have been," trust that what is unfolding may be far greater than what you imagined. Embracing the unexpected is a brave act of faith — it is believing that every detour, every surprise, is leading you exactly where you need to be.

🙏 Prayer

Heavenly Father,

Thank You for the plans You have for my life — plans that are good and full of hope. When I feel afraid or disappointed by unexpected changes, remind me that You are in control and that nothing surprises You. Help me release my need for certainty and embrace Your greater vision for my future. Fill me with peace, courage, and trust as I walk each new path. Amen.

💡 Practical Tips for Embracing the Unexpected

✅ **Begin each morning with surrender**: Pray, "Lord, guide me today. I trust Your plans above my own."

✅ **See challenges as opportunities**: Ask yourself, "What might God be teaching me through this change?"

✅ **Record hidden blessings**: Start a "God's surprises" journal to note ways God has worked through unexpected moments.

✅ **Focus on flexibility as strength**: Remind yourself that being adaptable does not mean giving up — it means growing.

✅ **Stay connected**: Lean on your support system when navigating life's surprises. You are not meant to go through this alone.

✍ Journaling Prompts

Write your reflections on the lines below. Take your time and be honest with yourself and with God.

1. Describe a time when something did not go according to plan but eventually led to unexpected blessings.

_____

_____

_____

_____

_____

2. How do you usually react when life surprises you? What would it look like to respond with faith instead of fear?

_____

_____

_____

_____

_____

3. What is one area of your life where you feel God might be inviting you to release control and trust Him more deeply?

_____

_____

_____

_____

_____

☘ Affirmation

"I release my plans and trust that God's unexpected paths lead me to beautiful places beyond my imagination."

💜 Reflection Space

CHAPTER 9

SMALL STEPS MATTER

In a world that often celebrates the grand and immediate, it is easy to overlook the quiet power of small, consistent steps. We live in an age of instant results, where social media highlights spectacular success stories that can make our own slow progress feel insignificant. But if you have ever felt like your efforts are too small to matter, know that you are not alone.

I remember feeling stuck during seasons when change seemed out of reach. Yet, looking back, those small, faithful choices — choosing patience, kindness, and trust day after day — laid the foundation for lasting growth. The truth is that every great accomplishment is built on a foundation of tiny actions.

Imagine planting a tree. It starts as a seed, invisible beneath the soil, slowly pushing roots deeper until it finally bursts into life. Your small steps are like that seed. Though invisible now, they are nurturing growth and preparing you for the future God has planned.

This chapter invites you to embrace your journey, honor every small victory, and trust that your consistent faithfulness matters more than you realize.

✨ Quotes

"Success is the sum of small efforts, repeated day in and day out."
— Robert Collier

"Great things are not done by impulse, but by a series of small things brought together."
— Vincent Van Gogh

"Little by little, a little becomes a lot."
— Tanzanian Proverb

🗨 Reflection

We often overlook the quiet progress happening in our lives because it lacks immediate glamour. But God sees every small act of love, every prayer whispered in silence, and every moment you resist giving up. He is building something beautiful through your daily choices.

Faithfulness in the trivial things builds endurance and shapes character. When we choose consistency over perfection, God uses that steady effort to prepare us for the blessings ahead. No step is wasted in His eyes.

If you are weary or discouraged, lean into the truth that growth often happens beneath the surface. Trust that your small steps will bloom into something greater with time.

🙏 Prayer
Lord,

Thank You for the power and purpose in every small step I take. Help me to remain faithful even when I cannot see immediate results. Strengthen my heart to keep moving forward with patience and trust in Your perfect timing. Remind me that You are working in and through my daily efforts. Amen.

💡 Practical Tips

- Break big goals into tiny, manageable steps.
- Celebrate your small victories daily.
- Keep a "small wins" journal to track progress.
- Share your journey with someone who encourages you.
- Practice patience and remind yourself growth takes time.

✍ Journaling Prompts

1. What small step have you taken recently that made a difference?

_____

_____

_____

_____

_____

2. How do you feel when progress seems slow or invisible?

_____

_____

_____

_____

3. What is one small step you can take today toward your goals or faith?

_____

_____

_____

_____

_____

❦ Affirmation

I honor and celebrate every small step I take. God is faithful to use them for His glory.

📖 Scripture

"Let us not become weary in doing good, for at the proper time we will reap a harvest if we do not give up."

— Galatians 6:9 (NIV)

♥ Reflection Space

_____
_____
_____
_____
_____
_____
_____
_____
_____
_____
_____
_____
_____
_____
_____
_____
_____
_____
_____
_____
_____
_____
_____
_____
_____
_____
_____
_____
_____
_____

CHAPTER 10

STRENGTH IN STILLNESS

In our busy, noisy world, stillness can feel like an unattainable luxury. We are encouraged to do more, be faster, and constantly produce. Yet, the wisdom of scripture invites us into quietness — a sacred pause where we can hear God's voice and find true strength.

Stillness is not emptiness or weakness. It is an intentional choice to stop striving, to rest in God's presence, and to open our hearts to His peace. I have experienced the power of stillness in my own life moments when stepping away from the chaos allowed God's peace to restore my soul and give me fresh courage to move forward.

This chapter invites you to discover the power and peace found in stillness, knowing that in quiet moments, God's strength is made perfect.

✦ Quotes

"Be still and know that I am God."
— Psalm 46:10

"Sometimes the most productive thing you can do is relax."
— Mark Black

"In the midst of movement and chaos, keep stillness inside of you."
— Deepak Chopra

💬 Reflection

We are often tempted to fill every moment with activity to avoid discomfort or uncertainty. But God calls us to stop, breathe, and simply be with Him. It is in these moments of stillness that we are renewed and reminded of His constant presence.

Stillness allows us to listen to God's whispers, calm our anxious thoughts, and center our hearts on His faithfulness. When we cultivate stillness, we develop resilience and a deep well of peace that sustains us through life's storms.

Challenge yourself today to embrace moments of quiet. Let stillness be a powerful act of faith, trusting God to work in ways beyond your understanding.

🛐 Prayer

Dear God,

Help me to slow down and be still in Your presence. When life feels overwhelming, draw me into Your peace. Quiet my restless heart and remind me that Your strength is made perfect in my weakness. Teach me to trust You in the silence. Amen.

💡 Practical Tips

- Schedule short daily quiet times to connect with God.
- Turn off screens and distractions during these moments.
- Practice deep breathing or meditation on scripture.
- Create a peaceful corner in your home for reflection.
- Use calming music or nature sounds to foster stillness.

✍ Journaling Prompts

1. What distractions keep you from being still?

_____

_____

_____

_____

_____

2. Describe a time when stillness brought you peace or clarity.

_____

_____

_____

_____

_____

3. How can you intentionally create more moments of stillness in your daily life?

_____

_____

_____

_____

_____

❡ Affirmation

In stillness, I find peace and strength. God is with me, even in the quiet.

📖 Scripture

"The Lord will fight for you; you need only to be still."
— Exodus 14:14 (NIV)

♥ Reflection Space

CHAPTER 11

COURAGE TO BEGIN AGAIN

Beginnings can be scary. Whether it is a new job, a new relationship, or a fresh start after failure or loss, stepping into the unknown takes courage. I have faced moments when starting over felt overwhelming — unsure if I had what it took to try again.

But I have also learned that every new beginning carries God's promise of hope and renewal. His mercies are new every morning, and He equips us with the strength and grace to begin again, no matter our past.

If you are feeling afraid to take a fresh step today, know you are not alone. This chapter is a gentle reminder that God's grace covers your fears and equips you with courage for the journey ahead.

✦ Quotes

"There is a crack in everything. That is how the light gets in."
— Leonard Cohen

"You are never too old to set another goal or to dream a new dream."
— C.S. Lewis

"The beginning is always today."
— Mary Shelley

💬 Reflection

Starting again is not failure — it is faith. It means you believe God is bigger than your past mistakes or setbacks. It means you trust His plan, even when the path ahead is uncertain.

God's grace is not just for forgiveness; it is for empowerment. It meets us where we are and gives us fresh strength to take that next step. I encourage you to embrace your new beginning with hope and confidence, knowing God is walking with you every step of the way.

Remember: you do not have to have it all figured out. Courage is moving forward even when you do not see the whole path.

🛐 Prayer

Gracious God,

Thank You for the gift of new beginnings. When fear or doubt hold me back, fill me with Your courage and hope. Help me to trust in Your plan and Your timing. Equip me to take each step with faith, knowing You are with me. Amen.

💡 Practical Tips

- Write down what you want to leave behind and what you want to embrace.
- Take one small step today toward your fresh start.
- Surround yourself with supportive, encouraging people.
- Keep a journal of your journey and prayers.
- Remember, progress is more important than perfection.

✍ Journaling Prompts

1. What new beginning are you longing or needing to start?

_____

_____

_____

_____

_____

2. What fears or doubts do you need to release to God?

_____

_____

_____

_____

3. Write a prayer asking God for courage to begin again.

_____

_____

_____

_____

❡ Affirmation

I am courageous and capable. God's grace empowers me to begin again.

📖 Scripture

"Therefore, if anyone is in Christ, the new creation has come: The old has gone, the new is here!"

— 2 Corinthians 5:17 (NIV)

💜 Reflection Space

CHAPTER 12

FINDING JOY IN THE JOURNEY

Joy is often misunderstood. Many think it is just happiness that depends on circumstances—sunny days, good news, celebrations. But real joy runs deeper. It is a steady current flowing through our souls, even when life is tough.

I have walked seasons where joy felt distant or impossible, yet when I intentionally focused on gratitude and God's faithfulness, joy found its way back to my heart. It is a choice to embrace God's goodness regardless of what is happening around us.

Joy is not a destination but a companion on the journey. It shines brightest when we choose to see blessings in the everyday moments—the smile of a stranger, a comforting word, the quiet beauty of nature.

This chapter invites you to discover how to cultivate joy daily, even amid trials, by anchoring your heart in God's unchanging love.

✦ Quotes

"Joy does not simply happen to us. We must choose joy and keep choosing it every day."
— Henri Nouwen

"Joy is the simplest form of gratitude."
— Karl Barth

"Find ecstasy in life; the mere sense of living is joy enough."
— Emily Dickinson

💬 Reflection

Joy is a discipline—a daily decision to see beyond circumstances and trust in God's goodness. It is not ignoring pain or difficulties but choosing to hold onto hope anyway.

When joy is rooted in faith, it becomes a wellspring of strength that carries us through hard days. Gratitude opens the door to joy, helping us notice the small miracles we might otherwise miss.

In your journey, look for those hidden sparks of joy and nurture them. Share them with others and watch how joy grows and transforms your perspective and your life.

🙏 Prayer
God of Joy,

Thank You for the gift of joy that transcends circumstances. Help me to choose joy daily, to focus on Your blessings and Your love. Fill my heart with laughter, peace, and hope. Teach me to share joy with those around me, so it multiplies and shines bright. Amen.

💡 Practical Tips
- Keep a daily gratitude journal listing three things you are thankful for.
- Surround yourself with joyful, positive influences.
- Practice smiling—even when you do not feel like it—to shift your mood.
- Listen to uplifting music or worship songs regularly.
- Serve others—joy grows when we give.

🔖 Journaling Prompts

1. What brings you joy in your daily life, big or small?

_____

_____

_____

_____

_____

2. How has joy helped you through tough times?

_____

_____

_____

_____

3. What can you do today to invite more joy into your life?

_____

_____

_____

_____

_____

🌱 Affirmation

I choose joy today and every day. God's love fills my heart with happiness and hope.

📖 Scripture

"Consider it pure joy, my brothers and sisters, whenever you face trials of many kinds, because you know that the testing of your faith produces perseverance."
— James 1:2-3 (NIV)

♥ Reflection Space

_____

_____

_____

_____

_____

_____

_____

_____

_____

_____

_____

_____

_____

_____

_____

_____

_____

_____

_____

_____

_____

_____

_____

_____

_____

_____

CHAPTER 13

GRACE IN THE STRUGGLE

Struggles are a natural part of life, but they can feel isolating, painful, and overwhelming. I have faced moments when the weight of my mistakes and hardships felt unbearable. Yet in those darkest times, God's grace revealed itself as my strongest anchor.

Grace is more than forgiveness; it is God's active, loving power meeting us in our brokenness and turning it into something new. When I learned to lean into grace instead of shame, I found freedom and healing.

This chapter invites you to embrace God's grace fully—not just when life is easy, but especially when it is hard. His grace covers our struggles and invites us to rise stronger.

✦ Quotes

"Grace means that all of your mistakes now serve a purpose instead of serving shame."
— Brené Brown

"God's grace is bigger than your mistakes."
— Unknown

"Grace is the face that love wears when it meets imperfection."
— Joseph R. Cooke

💬 Reflection

It is tempting to let our struggles define us, but God's grace says otherwise. His love meets us in our weaknesses and transforms them. When we accept grace, we stop carrying the heavy burden of shame and step into freedom.

Grace also teaches us to be gentle with ourselves and others. It is a healing balm that restores hope and encourages growth. No matter what you face, God's grace is enough to carry you through.

🛕 Prayer
Merciful God,

Thank You for Your amazing grace that meets me in my struggles. When I feel weak or broken, remind me that Your grace is sufficient. Help me to accept Your love fully and to extend grace to myself and others. Heal my heart and renew my strength. Amen.

💡 Practical Tips

- Practice self-compassion—speak kindly to yourself.
- Memorize grace-filled scriptures for encouragement.
- Reach out for support from trusted friends or mentors.
- Write down lessons you have learned through struggles.
- Celebrate small victories and progress.

✍ Journaling Prompts

1. How have you experienced God's grace during tough times?

_____
_____
_____
_____
_____

2. What burdens or mistakes do you need to give over to God's grace?

_____
_____
_____
_____

3. How can you practice grace toward yourself and others today?

_____
_____
_____
_____
_____

❣ Affirmation

God's grace is enough for me. I am loved, forgiven, and made new.

📖 Scripture

"My grace is sufficient for you, for my power is made perfect in weakness."
— 2 Corinthians 12:9 (NIV)

♥ Reflection Space

CHAPTER 14

HOPE ANCHORED IN FAITH

Hope can feel fragile in a world full of uncertainty, but when rooted in faith, it becomes a powerful anchor for the soul. I have faced seasons where hope seemed distant, yet holding fast to God's promises kept me grounded and steady.

Hope is not blind optimism or denial of hardship; it is confident trust in God's goodness and faithfulness even when the path is unclear. This chapter invites you to anchor your hope firmly in God, knowing He is a constant presence through every storm.

When hope and faith work together, they create resilience—a courage to face life's challenges with peace and expectation for what is ahead.

✦ Quotes

"We have this hope as an anchor for the soul, firm and secure."
— Hebrews 6:19

"Hope is the only thing stronger than fear."
— Suzanne Collins

"Faith is the bird that feels the light when the dawn is still dark."
— Rabindranath Tagore

💬 Reflection

Hope grounded in faith is unshakable. It holds us steady when circumstances shake us to our core. When we place our trust in God's promises, we receive a peace that transcends understanding.

I encourage you to build your hope on the firm foundation of God's word. Remember His faithfulness in your life and cling to the assurance that He is working all things for good.

No matter what you face today, God's hope is a steady anchor that will not fail you.

🙏 Prayer

God of Hope,

Thank You for being my anchor in every storm. When I feel overwhelmed or uncertain, help me to trust You fully. Strengthen my faith so that my hope stays firm and unshaken. Guide me to share hope with those who need it, reflecting Your light. Amen.

💡 Practical Tips

- Memorize key scripture promises about hope and faith.
- Surround yourself with encouraging, faith-filled people.
- Keep a journal of God's faithfulness in your life.
- Speak hope aloud in difficult moments.
- Use worship and prayer to renew your hope daily.

✍ Journaling Prompts

1. When has hope helped you through a difficult season?

_____

_____

_____

_____

_____

2. What promises from God do you cling to when hope feels distant?

_____

_____

_____

_____

3. How can you share hope with someone else today?

_____

_____

_____

_____

ϒ Affirmation

My hope is anchored in God's faithfulness. He is my steady rock and refuge.

📖 Scripture

"May the God of hope fill you with all joy and peace as you trust in Him."
— Romans 15:13 (NIV)

❤️ Reflection Space

CHAPTER 15

LIGHT IN THE DARKNESS

Darkness can come in many forms: grief, disappointment, loneliness, anxiety. In those moments, it feels like the light has disappeared, leaving us to navigate an endless night. I have faced such seasons myself — times when I questioned if I would ever feel joy or peace again.

But I have discovered that even the darkest night cannot extinguish the light of God's love. His light breaks through our deepest pain, offering hope and guidance. It may not remove every struggle instantly, but it gives us the strength to keep moving forward, one step at a time.

This chapter invites you to find and hold onto the light, no matter how small it may seem. God's light is always shining — sometimes as a bright sunrise, other times as a single candle in the dark.

You do not have to find your way alone. God is with you, ready to illuminate each step and lead you toward healing and new life.

✦ Quotes

"The light shines in the darkness, and the darkness has not overcome it."
— John 1:5

"Hope is being able to see that there is light despite all of the darkness."
— Desmond Tutu

"Stars can't shine without darkness."
— D.H. Sidebottom

💬 Reflection

Even when we cannot see it, light is always present. Our eyes just need time to adjust. In life, we often find ourselves in situations that feel hopeless, but God's love shines quietly, calling us to trust.

When we fix our eyes on His promises, we notice His light guiding us. It may come as an encouraging word, an unexpected blessing, or a deep sense of peace in the middle of chaos.

If you are facing darkness now, remember that the light is closer than you think. Hold on and let God's love illuminate your heart.

🙏 Prayer

Dear Lord,

Thank You for being my light in every dark season. When I feel lost or overwhelmed, help me to fix my eyes on You. Shine Your light into the hidden corners of my heart and guide me toward hope and healing. Thank You for never leaving me in the dark alone. Amen.

💡 Practical Tips

- Write down scriptures or quotes about light and keep them visible.
- Light a candle during prayer or journaling as a visual reminder of God's presence.
- Spend time outside in natural light to uplift your spirit.
- Create a gratitude list focused on small "lights" in your life.
- Seek support from trusted friends or a faith community.

✍ Journaling Prompts

1. When have you experienced God's light during a tough time?

_____

_____

_____

_____

_____

2. What areas of your life feel dark or uncertain right now?

_____

_____

_____

_____

3. How can you invite more light into your daily routine?

_____

_____

_____

_____

❦ Affirmation

God's light shines in me and through me. I am never alone in the darkness.

📖 Scripture

"Your word is a lamp for my feet, a light on my path."
— Psalm 119:105 (NIV)

♥ Reflection Space

_____

_____

_____

_____

_____

_____

_____

_____

_____

_____

_____

_____

_____

_____

_____

_____

_____

_____

_____

_____

_____

_____

_____

_____

_____

_____

CHAPTER 16

TRUSTING THE PROCESS

We live in a world that celebrates instant results. We want quick answers, rapid growth, and immediate solutions. But the truth is, life is a journey of process. God often works slowly, shaping us through seasons of waiting, stretching, and refining.

There have been times when I felt stuck, wondering if God had forgotten me. Yet looking back, I see those were the moments He was building my faith and character most deeply.

Trusting the process means believing that even when we cannot see progress, God is working behind the scenes. It means surrendering our timelines and leaning into His perfect plan, step by step.

This chapter invites you to let go of impatience and embrace the beautiful unfolding of God's work in your life.

✦ Quotes

"Trust the process. Your time is coming. Just do the work and the results will handle themselves."
— Tony Gaskins

"God's timing is perfect. Trust His delays. He has you."
— Unknown

"Faith is trusting God even when you don't understand His plan."
— Unknown

💬 Reflection

It is easy to feel discouraged when we do not see immediate results. But often, the greatest transformations happen underground, hidden from view. Like seeds growing roots before breaking through the soil, God prepares us in unseen ways.

Trusting the process requires patience and faith. It asks us to release control and choose trust over anxiety. Remember that God is never in a hurry, and His ways are higher and wiser than ours.

When you feel stuck, remind yourself that this season has a purpose. Keep showing up, keep believing, and watch as God weaves your story into something beautiful.

🙏 Prayer
Faithful Father,

Thank You for working in my life even when I cannot see it. Teach me to trust Your timing and to rest in Your promises. Give me patience in the waiting and strength to keep moving forward. Help me to surrender my plans and embrace Your perfect process. Amen.

💡 Practical Tips

- Reflect on past seasons where God came through after waiting.
- Create a "trust journal" where you write prayers and answered prayers.
- Practice daily surrender in prayer, releasing specific worries.
- Repeat faith-based affirmations during anxious moments.
- Celebrate small milestones along the way.

✍ Journaling Prompts

1. Where in your life do you struggle most to trust the process?

_____

_____

_____

_____

_____

2. How has God shown His faithfulness to you in the past?

_____

_____

_____

_____

_____

3. What would it look like to fully surrender this area to God today?

_____

_____

_____

_____

_____

✝ Affirmation

I trust God's process for my life. His timing is perfect, and His plan is good.

📖 Scripture

"Being confident of this, that he who began a good work in you will carry it on to completion until the day of Christ Jesus."
— Philippians 1:6 (NIV)

💗 Reflection Space

CHAPTER 17

WALKING IN FORGIVENESS

Forgiveness is one of the most challenging and freeing acts we can choose. Holding onto anger or hurt can weigh us down and rob us of peace. Yet, forgiveness is not about excusing someone's behavior — it is about setting your own heart free.

I have experienced the struggle of letting go. Sometimes the wounds run deep, and it feels impossible to release the pain. But in those moments, God's grace offers us strength to forgive, just as we have been forgiven.

Choosing forgiveness is an act of courage and faith. It is a daily decision that brings healing and opens the door to new beginnings.

This chapter invites you to experience the power of forgiveness and the freedom it brings to your soul.

✦ Quotes

"To forgive is to set a prisoner free and discover that the prisoner was you."
— Lewis B. Smedes

"Forgiveness is not an occasional act; it is a constant attitude."
— Martin Luther King Jr.

"Forgiveness does not change the past, but it does enlarge the future."
— Paul Boese

💬 Reflection

Forgiveness is a process, not a one-time event. It might take time and repeated choices, but each step moves you closer to freedom.

God does not ask us to forgive in our own strength. He offers us His grace and compassion to help us release bitterness and pain.

When we walk in forgiveness, we make room for peace, joy, and restoration. We can let go of the past and step into the fullness of life God has for us.

🙏 Prayer

Lord of Mercy,

Thank You for forgiving me and teaching me to forgive others. Give me the strength to release every hurt and every offense into Your hands. Heal my heart and replace bitterness with Your love. Help me to walk in freedom and grace every day. Amen.

💡 Practical Tips

- Write a letter expressing your feelings (you do not have to send it).
- Pray daily for those who hurt you, asking God to bless them.
- Focus on your own healing and growth rather than revenge.
- Reflect on God's forgiveness toward you as inspiration.
- Set healthy boundaries to protect your heart.

🖋 Journaling Prompts

1. Who do you need to forgive, and why is it difficult?

_____

_____

_____

_____

_____

2. How has holding onto unforgiveness affected your life?

_____

_____

_____

_____

3. What would it feel like to finally release this burden to God?

_____

_____

_____

_____

🕯 Affirmation

I choose to forgive and set myself free. God's love heals and restores my heart.

📖 Scripture

"Be kind and compassionate to one another, forgiving each other, just as in Christ God forgave you."

— Ephesians 4:32 (NIV)

❤️ Reflection Space

CHAPTER 18

LETTING GO AND MOVING FORWARD

Letting go is one of the hardest, yet most liberating, choices we can make. Whether it is releasing an old dream, a toxic relationship, a painful past, or control over a situation — letting go opens the door to new blessings and fresh starts.

I have learned that holding tightly to what no longer serves us can prevent us from receiving God's new gifts. When we let go, we make space for growth, healing, and unexpected joy.

This chapter invites you to trust God with what you are releasing and to step boldly into the future He has for you.

Remember: you are not losing; you are creating space for something better.

✦ Quotes

"Sometimes letting things go is an act of far greater power than defending or hanging on."
— Eckhart Tolle

"You will find that it is necessary to let things go; simply for the reason that they are heavy."
— C. JoyBell C.

"Let go and let God."
— Unknown

💬 Reflection

Letting go is not about giving up — it is about surrendering control and trusting God's greater plan. It means believing that His ways are better than ours and that He is faithful to lead us into something new and good.

As you release what weighs you down, you will find freedom and peace that surpasses understanding. Moving forward becomes possible when we stop clinging to the past.

God promises to be with you every step of the way. Trust Him as you let go and look ahead with hope and expectancy.

🎧 Prayer

Loving Father,

I surrender everything I am holding onto today. Help me to release it fully into Your hands. Give me courage to move forward and faith to trust that You have something better for me. Fill my heart with peace and hope for what is ahead. Amen.

💡 Practical Tips

- Make a list of things you need to let go of and pray over each one.
- Practice breathing exercises to help release emotional tension.
- Surround yourself with supportive friends who encourage growth.
- Set new goals or dreams to focus your energy forward.
- Create a symbolic act (like writing and burning a letter) to mark the release.

✍ Journaling Prompts

1. What do you feel God is calling you to let go of?

_____

_____

_____

_____

2. What new opportunities could open if you released it?

_____

_____

_____

3. What does moving forward look like for you?

_____

_____

_____

_____

ⵗ Affirmation

I let go and trust God to lead me forward. My future is full of hope and new beginnings.

📖 Scripture

"Forget the former things; do not dwell on the past. See, I am doing a new thing!"
— Isaiah 43:18-19 (NIV)

♥ Reflection Space

_____

_____

_____

_____

_____

_____

_____

_____

_____

_____

_____

_____

_____

_____

_____

_____

_____

_____

_____

_____

_____

_____

_____

_____

_____

_____

_____

_____

_____

CHAPTER 19

PURPOSE IN EVERY SEASON

Life moves through seasons — times of growth, harvest, rest, and even pruning. Each season has its own lessons, challenges, and blessings. We often celebrate the seasons of abundance but struggle with the seasons of waiting or loss. Yet, every season holds purpose when we walk with God.

I have experienced times when it felt like nothing was moving forward, where doors closed and dreams seemed on hold. But looking back, those seasons prepared me for future growth in ways I could never have imagined. God wastes nothing; every moment is part of His divine plan.

This chapter invites you to embrace each season with openness and trust. Even when it feels uncomfortable or confusing, remember God is working behind the scenes, shaping you for what is next.

You are exactly where you need to be for this moment. Trust that He is using every season to bring you closer to your purpose.

✦ Quotes

"To everything there is a season, and a time for every purpose under heaven."
— Ecclesiastes 3:1

"Bloom where you are planted."
— Saint Francis de Sales

"Every season serves a purpose. Even the ones that seem barren can bring forth new life."
— Unknown

💬 Reflection

Seasons of life can feel unpredictable, but each one is necessary for growth. The quiet, unseen seasons build roots. The blooming seasons reveal beauty and joy. The harvest seasons celebrate challenging work, and the pruning seasons refine and strengthen us.

Instead of fighting against where you are, lean in and ask God what He wants to teach you now. Trust that He is preparing you, even in ways you cannot see.

Embrace the process, knowing each season is a steppingstone toward the greater purpose God has for your life.

🙏 Prayer

Heavenly Father,

Thank You for being with me in every season of my life. Help me to trust Your timing and to learn the lessons You have for me in each stage. Give me patience during waiting, joy during growth, and strength during pruning. Remind me that You are always working for my good. Amen.

💡 Practical Tips

- Identify what season of life you are in right now and reflect on its purpose.
- Journal about the blessings and lessons of this season.
- Seek God's guidance daily, asking what He wants you to focus on today.
- Avoid comparing your season to others — your journey is unique.
- Celebrate small milestones and growth.

✍ Journaling Prompts

1. What season of life are you currently in? How does it feel?

_____

_____

_____

_____

_____

2. What might God be teaching you in this season?

_____

_____

_____

_____

3. How can you make the most of this season with faith and gratitude?

_____

_____

_____

_____

❦ Affirmation

I embrace every season of my life, knowing God has a purpose and plan for each one.

📖 Scripture

"And we know that in all things God works for the good of those who love him, who have been called according to his purpose."

— Romans 8:28 (NIV)

♥ Reflection Space

CHAPTER 20

FINDING YOUR TRUE IDENTITY

Who am I? It is a question we all wrestle with at some point. In a world filled with labels, expectations, and comparisons, it is easy to lose sight of our identity. We define ourselves by roles, achievements, or failures, forgetting who God says we are.

I have struggled with self-worth and identity, chasing validation from people and accomplishments. But real peace and confidence came when I began to root my identity in Christ alone.

God created each of us uniquely, intentionally, and lovingly. Our true worth does not come from what we do but from who we belong to.

This chapter invites you to rediscover your identity as God's beloved child. You are chosen, cherished, and enough just as you are.

✦ Quotes

"You are God's masterpiece, created in Christ Jesus to do good works."
— Ephesians 2:10

"Define yourself radically as one beloved by God. This is the true self."
— Brennan Manning

"You are enough, simply because you are His."
— Unknown

💬 Reflection

When we seek identity from the world, we end up feeling empty and exhausted. But when we anchor our identity in God's love, we find freedom and rest.

Your value does not depend on your past mistakes or future successes. You are valuable because God says so. You were created with purpose, and nothing can change that truth.

Embrace your identity as His child and live with the confidence and joy that come from knowing you are deeply loved.

🎧 Prayer

Loving Father,

Thank You for creating me uniquely and calling me Your beloved. Help me to see myself through Your eyes and to reject any lies about my worth. Root my identity deeply in Your love so I can live boldly and freely. Amen.

💡 Practical Tips

- Write affirmations about your identity in Christ and read them daily.
- Surround yourself with people who remind you of your worth.
- Avoid comparing yourself to others; celebrate your uniqueness.
- Reflect on scripture that affirms your identity.
- Spend time in prayer asking God to reveal His vision for you.

📖 Journaling Prompts

1. How have you defined yourself in the past, and how did it affect you?

_____

_____

_____

_____

2. What does God say about your identity?

_____

_____

_____

3. What would change in your life if you fully embraced your identity as His beloved?

_____

_____

_____

_____

🌱 Affirmation

I am chosen, loved, and enough. My identity is secure in Christ alone.

📖 Scripture

"See what great love the Father has lavished on us, that we should be called children of God! And that is what we are!"

— 1 John 3:1 (NIV)

♥ Reflection Space

CHAPTER 21

LIVING WITH GRATITUDE

Gratitude is more than a polite "thank you;" it is a powerful posture of the heart that transforms how we see life. When we choose gratitude, we shift our focus from what is missing to what is present.

I have had seasons when gratitude felt hard to find. But even in tough times, there were blessings — a supportive friend, a warm meal, a moment of laughter. Gratitude does not deny pain; it simply helps us see that God's goodness is always present.

A grateful heart attracts joy, fosters contentment, and strengthens faith. When we live with gratitude, we become more aware of God's constant provision and love.

This chapter invites you to cultivate a habit of gratitude, transforming your perspective and deepening your relationship with God.

✦ Quotes

"Gratitude turns what we have into enough."
— Melody Beattie

"Give thanks to the Lord, for He is good; His love endures forever."
— Psalm 107:1

"When I started counting my blessings, my whole life turned around."
— Willie Nelson

💬 Reflection

Gratitude is a daily choice. It may not always feel natural, but with practice, it can become a way of life. When we give thanks in all circumstances, we open our eyes to the blessings that surround us.

Practicing gratitude draws us closer to God, reminding us of His faithfulness and love. Even small expressions of thankfulness can create ripples of joy and peace throughout our lives.

Start today — find one thing to thank God for and watch how it transforms your heart.

🙏 Prayer

Gracious God,

Thank You for every blessing You have poured into my life. Help me to see Your goodness in every moment, even the challenging ones. Teach me to live with a heart full of gratitude and to share that thankfulness with others. Amen.

💡 Practical Tips

- Keep a gratitude journal and write three things each day you are thankful for.
- Start and end each day with a short prayer of thanks.
- Verbally express appreciation to people around you.
- Create visual reminders (like sticky notes) to focus on blessings.
- Celebrate small wins and moments of joy.

✍ Journaling Prompts

1. What blessings in your life have you overlooked lately?

_____

_____

_____

_____

_____

2. How has gratitude shifted your perspective in the past?

_____

_____

_____

_____

3. What are you most grateful for today?

_____

_____

_____

_____

♈ Affirmation

My heart is full of gratitude. I see and celebrate God's goodness every day.

📖 Scripture

"Give thanks in all circumstances; for this is God's will for you in Christ Jesus."
— 1 Thessalonians 5:18 (NIV)

❤️ Reflection Space

CHAPTER 22

UNSHAKEABLE PEACE

Peace is one of the most precious gifts God offers us. Yet, in a world filled with noise, chaos, and uncertainty, it can feel impossible to find. True peace is not found in perfect circumstances; it is found in the presence of God.

I have struggled with anxiety and restlessness, searching for peace in control, achievements, or distractions. But real, unshakeable peace came when I learned to rest in God's promises and trust Him fully.

This chapter invites you to discover the peace that surpasses understanding — a peace that remains steady even in storms.

God's peace is not temporary; it is a lasting assurance that no matter what happens around you, He holds you securely.

✦ Quotes

"Peace, I leave with you; my peace I give you."
— John 14:27

"You will keep in perfect peace those whose minds are steadfast, because they trust in you."
— Isaiah 26:3

"Peace is not the absence of trouble, but the presence of Christ."
— Unknown

💬 Reflection

True peace begins when we surrender our worries to God and anchor our hearts in His truth. It does not mean we will not face challenges, but it means we can move through them with calm assurance.

When anxiety rises, returning to God's word and promises brings calm and strength. By focusing on His constant love and faithfulness, we can experience peace during chaos.

Today, choose to lean into His peace. Let it fill your heart and mind and become a light to those around you.

🛐 Prayer

Prince of Peace,

Thank You for offering me a peace that surpasses all understanding. Help me to trust You fully and to rest in Your presence when life feels overwhelming. Guard my heart and mind with Your perfect peace and guide me each day. Amen.

💡 Practical Tips

- Meditate on scriptures about peace each morning.
- Practice breath prayers (inhale: "God is with me," exhale: "I am at peace").
- Create a calming routine before bed to quiet your mind.
- Limit negative news and media to protect your peace.
- Spend time in nature to connect with God's tranquility.

✍ Journaling Prompts

1. What situations tend to steal your peace?

_____

_____

_____

_____

_____

2. How do you feel when you experience God's peace?

_____

_____

_____

_____

3. What steps can you take today to invite more peace into your life?

_____

_____

_____

_____

_____

❯ Affirmation

I am filled with God's unshakeable peace. My heart rests securely in Him.

📖 Scripture

"And the peace of God, which transcends all understanding, will guard your hearts and your minds in Christ Jesus."

— Philippians 4:7 (NIV)

❤️ Reflection Space

CHAPTER 23

STRENGTH IN WEAKNESS

We live in a world that often tells us to hide our weaknesses and always present a strong front. But God invites us to a unique way — a way where our weakness becomes the very place His strength shines brightest.

I have had moments when my own strength was not enough — when fear, doubt, or exhaustion took over. In those moments, I discovered the truth of God's promise: His strength is made perfect in our weakness.

This chapter invites you to stop striving for perfection and start embracing your need for God. When we lean into Him, we find a strength that goes beyond what we could ever muster alone.

Your weakness is not a flaw; it is an opportunity to experience God's power and grace in new, beautiful ways.

✦ Quotes

"My grace is sufficient for you, for my power is made perfect in weakness."
— 2 Corinthians 12:9

"God does not give us overcoming life — He gives us life as we overcome."
— Oswald Chambers

"Our strength grows out of our weaknesses."
— Ralph Waldo Emerson

💬 Reflection

It is in the broken, fragile places of our lives that God does His greatest work. When we acknowledge our dependence on Him, we open ourselves to His limitless strength.

Instead of hiding or resenting your weaknesses, invite God into them. Watch as He turns your moments of struggle into testimonies of His love and power.

Remember: your weakness does not disqualify you; it qualifies you to receive His grace in full.

🙏 Prayer

Mighty God,

Thank You for loving me in my weakness and for being my strength. Help me to stop relying on my own power and to trust fully in You. Teach me to see my weaknesses as opportunities to draw closer to You and to testify to Your greatness. Amen.

💡 Practical Tips

- When feeling weak, pause to pray instead of pushing through alone.
- Memorize scriptures that remind you of God's strength.
- Share your struggles with a trusted friend or mentor for support.
- Reflect on past moments when God's strength carried you.
- Celebrate small victories as reminders of His help.

✍ Journaling Prompts

1. What weaknesses are you most afraid to show or admit?

_____

_____

_____

_____

_____

2. How has God shown His strength through your challenges?

_____

_____

_____

_____

3. In what areas of your life can you invite God's strength today?

_____

_____

_____

_____

⍦ Affirmation

God's strength is made perfect in my weakness. I am strong in Him.

📖 Scripture

"The Lord is my strength and my shield; my heart trusts in him, and he helps me."
— Psalm 28:7 (NIV)

♥ Reflection Space

CHAPTER 24

THE POWER OF PRAYER

Prayer is not just a religious duty; it is a lifeline, a constant invitation to connect with the heart of God. It is in prayer that we pour out our worries, express our gratitude, find guidance, and experience peace beyond understanding.

I used to see prayer as a checklist or a ritual, but over time, I discovered it is much more — it is a relationship. It is where I learned to hear God's gentle whispers, to surrender my fears, and to receive strength for the journey.

This chapter invites you to deepen your prayer life, not as a task, but as a sacred conversation with your loving Father.

Prayer changes things — and even more, it changes us.

✦ Quotes

"Prayer is simply talking to God like a friend and should be the easiest thing we do each day."
— Joyce Meyer

"To be a Christian without prayer is no more possible than to be alive without breathing."
— Martin Luther

"God shapes the world by prayer."
— E.M. Bounds

💬 Reflection

Prayer is powerful because it connects us directly to the source of life and love. It is not about saying the perfect words but opening your heart honestly.

Through prayer, we discover God's heart for us, gain wisdom for decisions, and receive comfort during pain. Even when prayers seem unanswered, God is working in ways we might not see yet.

Make prayer your first response, not your last resort. Let it become the foundation of every day and every moment.

🎧 Prayer

Heavenly Father,

Thank You for always listening to me and for welcoming me into Your presence. Teach me to pray with honesty and faith. Help me to trust that You hear every word and are always working for my good. Strengthen my relationship with You through prayer. Amen.

💡 Practical Tips

- Start each morning with a short prayer of gratitude and surrender.
- Set reminders throughout the day to pause and talk to God.
- Keep a prayer journal to track requests and answered prayers.
- Pray scripture passages to deepen connection and understanding.
- Join a prayer group or pray with a friend for accountability.

✍ Journaling Prompts

1. What does prayer currently look like in your life?

_____

_____

_____

_____

_____

2. How has prayer affected you during difficult seasons?

_____

_____

_____

_____

3. What is one area you want to grow in your prayer life?

_____

_____

_____

_____

ⵆ Affirmation

I am deeply connected to God through prayer. My heart is open, and my faith is strong.

📖 Scripture

"The prayer of a righteous person is powerful and effective."
— James 5:16 (NIV)

💝 Reflection Space

CHAPTER 25

THE BLESSING OF COMMUNITY

God never intended for us to walk through life alone. We are created for connection, for relationships that encourage, support, and challenge us to grow. Community is a gift that strengthens our faith and reminds us that we are loved and seen.

There were times when I tried to handle life's struggles by myself, thinking it was a sign of strength. But I learned that true strength is found in vulnerability and allowing others to walk beside us.

This chapter invites you to embrace the blessing of community — to lean on others and to be a source of light and love in return.

Together, we reflect God's love in a powerful way.

✦ Quotes

"Carry each other's burdens, and in this way, you will fulfill the law of Christ."
— Galatians 6:2

"Alone we can do so little; together we can do so much."
— Helen Keller

"Community is where humility and glory touch."
— Henri Nouwen

💬 Reflection

When we open our hearts to community, we experience God's love in tangible ways. We learn from each other's stories, find comfort in shared struggles, and celebrate victories together.

Community does not have to be large; it can be a few trusted friends, a small group, or even a supportive family. The key is to be real, to show up for others, and to let them show up for you.

God often uses relationships to heal and grow us. Do not miss this beautiful gift.

🛐 Prayer

Loving God,

Thank You for the gift of community and the people You have placed in my life. Help me to be open, vulnerable, and loving. Teach me to support others and allow them to support me. May my relationships reflect Your love and bring You glory. Amen.

💡 Practical Tips

- Reach out to a friend or family member today and check in genuinely.
- Join a small group or community gathering to build deeper connections.
- Be intentional about both giving and receiving support.
- Practice active listening and empathy in your interactions.
- Pray regularly for your community and its needs.

✍ Journaling Prompts

1. Who are the people in your life that make up your community?

____

____

____

____

____

2. How have you seen God work through your relationships?

____

____

____

____

____

3. What steps can you take to nurture and grow your community?

____

____

____

____

____

Affirmation

I am blessed with a loving community. Together, we grow stronger and reflect God's love.

🕮 Scripture

"For where two or three gather in my name, there am I with them."
— Matthew 18:20 (NIV)

❤️ Reflection Space

CHAPTER 26

BECOMING A LIGHT TO OTHERS

We are called not only to receive God's love but to share it — to be a light in a world that desperately needs hope and kindness. Each of us carries a unique light that can brighten someone else's darkness.

I have learned that being a light does not always mean doing grand gestures. Sometimes it is a smile, a word of encouragement, a helping hand, or simply being present.

This chapter invites you to shine your light boldly, knowing that even the smallest acts of love can have a profound impact.

God shines through you — let that light reach everywhere.

✨ Quotes

"Let your light shine before others, that they may see your good deeds and glorify your Father in heaven."
— Matthew 5:16

"A candle loses nothing by lighting another candle."
— James Keller

"You are the light of the world."
— Matthew 5:14

💬 Reflection

Being a light means living authentically, reflecting God's love through our actions and words. It is about being kind when it is hard, forgiving quickly, and loving unconditionally.

Your light may be the only glimpse of God someone sees today. Use it to uplift, inspire, and bring hope wherever you go.

Trust that even small acts matter. You never know whose life you may touch.

🙏 Prayer

Lord of Light,

Thank You for filling me with Your love and truth. Help me to be a shining light to those around me. Guide my actions and words so they reflect Your heart. Use me to bring hope, joy, and encouragement to the world. Amen.

💡 Practical Tips

- Perform random acts of kindness throughout your week.
- Offer a listening ear to someone who needs it.
- Share your story of faith and hope with someone new.
- Volunteer or serve in your local community.
- Speak words of affirmation and encouragement daily.

✎ Journaling Prompts

1. Who has been a light in your life, and what impact did they have?

_____

_____

_____

_____

_____

2. How can you shine your light in your community or family?

_____

_____

_____

_____

3. What small acts of kindness can you commit to this week?

_____

_____

_____

_____

❦ Affirmation

I am a light in this world. God's love shines through me to touch others.

📖 Scripture

"Arise, shine, for your light has come, and the glory of the Lord rises upon you."
— Isaiah 60:1 (NIV)

❤️ Reflection Space

CHAPTER 27

TRUSTING GOD'S TIMING

We live in a world that glorifies instant results — fast food, quick fixes, overnight success. But God's timing often does not match ours. His plans unfold slowly, beautifully, and purposefully.

There were many times when I felt impatient with God. I wanted answers now, doors to open at once, healing to come overnight. But looking back, I see that His timing was always perfect. What seemed like delays were divine preparations.

This chapter invites you to surrender your timeline and trust that God's timing is always for your good. Even when it feels slow, He is never late.

✦ Quotes

"God's timing is always perfect. Trust His delays. He has you."
— Unknown

"Wait for the LORD; be strong and take heart and wait for the LORD."
— Psalm 27:14

"Faith in God includes faith in His timing."
— Neal A. Maxwell

💬 Reflection

Trusting God's timing is an act of surrender. It means believing that He sees the bigger picture and knows what is best for us, even when we do not understand.

When we rush ahead, we miss the growth that comes in the waiting. God uses seasons of waiting to strengthen our faith, refine our character, and prepare us for what is next.

Take a deep breath today and remember: He is working in ways you cannot see.

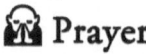 Prayer

Faithful Father,

Help me to trust Your timing even when I feel impatient. Teach me to rest in Your promises and to wait with a hopeful heart. Strengthen my faith as I learn to rely on Your perfect plan. Amen.

💡 Practical Tips

- Write down times when God's timing turned out better than your own.
- Practice gratitude while you wait.
- Repeat a breath prayer: "I trust Your timing, Lord."
- Avoid comparing your journey to others.
- Find joy in the present moment instead of rushing to the future.

✍ Journaling Prompts

1. What are you currently waiting on God for?

_____

_____

_____

_____

_____

2. How has waiting shaped your faith in the past?

_____

_____

_____

_____

3. What might God be teaching you in this season of waiting?

_____

_____

_____

_____

❦ Affirmation

I trust God's perfect timing. I am exactly where I need to be.

📖 Scripture

"There is a time for everything, and a season for every activity under the heavens."
— Ecclesiastes 3:1

❤️ Reflection Space

CHAPTER 28

HEALING FROM THE PAST

Our past can feel like a heavy weight — mistakes, regrets, hurts we did not ask for. But God does not want us to live in the shadow of yesterday. He invites us into freedom and healing.

I have carried wounds that felt impossible to heal. But through faith, prayer, and God's gentle love, I found restoration and a new identity in Him.

This chapter invites you to release what is behind you and embrace the new thing God is doing in your life.

✦ Quotes

"Forget the former things; do not dwell on the past. See, I am doing a new thing!"
— Isaiah 43:18–19

"Scars are proof that you survived and that God heals."
— Unknown

"You cannot start the next chapter if you keep re-reading the last one."
— Unknown

💬 Reflection

Healing does not mean forgetting. It means finding peace and allowing God to transform your pain into purpose.

Release your past into God's hands. Allow Him to mend the broken pieces and create something beautiful. You are not defined by what happened to you but by who He says you are.

🙏 Prayer

Healer of my soul,

I surrender my past to You. Heal my wounds, restore my joy, and help me step into the future You have prepared for me. Thank You for Your mercy and grace that make me new each day. Amen.

💡 Practical Tips

- Write a letter to your past self, offering forgiveness and compassion.
- Practice daily affirmations of your new identity in Christ.
- Surround yourself with supportive, faith-filled community.
- Seek counseling or pastoral support if needed.
- Reflect on and celebrate how far you have come.

✍ Journaling Prompts

1. What parts of your past still hold power over you?

_____

_____

_____

_____

_____

2. What does healing look like for you?

_____

_____

_____

_____

_____

3. What new thing might God want to do in your life today?

_____

_____

_____

_____

_____

☿ Affirmation

I am healed and free. My past no longer defines me.

📖 Scripture

"Therefore, if anyone is in Christ, the new creation has come: The old has gone, the new is here!"

— 2 Corinthians 5:17

❤ Reflection Space

CHAPTER 29

DISCOVERING JOY IN THE EVERYDAY

Joy is not just a feeling reserved for big celebrations. It is a choice we can make every day, even in ordinary moments.

I used to wait for extraordinary events or major milestones to feel joyful. But I have learned that true joy is found in the simple, often unnoticed moments — a sunrise, a kind word, a shared laugh.

This chapter invites you to open your eyes and heart to the joy that surrounds you daily. God wants you to live with a joy that cannot be shaken by circumstances.

✦ Quotes

"The joy of the Lord is your strength."
— Nehemiah 8:10

"Joy is not in things; it is in us."
— Richard Wagner

"Find joy in the journey."
— Unknown

💬 Reflection

Joy flows from gratitude, not circumstances. When we slow down and look for God's blessings in each day, we find endless reasons to smile.

Choosing joy transforms our perspective, relationships, and faith. It reminds us that God is present in every detail of our lives.

🛐 Prayer

Joyful God,

Help me to see and savor the joy in my daily life. Teach me to find beauty in trivial things and to rejoice in Your constant goodness. Let my heart overflow with Your joy today. Amen.

💡 Practical Tips

- Start a daily joy journal.
- Be available for things that bring you life and laughter.
- Share joy by encouraging someone else.
- Notice and give thanks for small blessings.
- Practice smiling — it lifts your spirit and others.'

✍ Journaling Prompts

1. What brings you joy on a normal day?

_____

_____

_____

_____

_____

2. How can you choose joy during tough times?

_____

_____

_____

_____

3. What small joys are you thankful for today?

_____

_____

_____

_____

❦ Affirmation

I choose joy today and every day. My heart is full and grateful.

📖 Scripture

"Rejoice always."

— 1 Thessalonians 5:16

♥ Reflection Space

CHAPTER 30

RESTING IN GOD'S PRESENCE

In a world that demands constant movement and productivity, rest often feels like a luxury instead of a necessity. But God calls us to rest — to pause, breathe, and be refreshed in His presence.

I have experienced burnout from striving and overworking. In those moments, I discovered the beauty of simply being still with God. His presence restores us in ways no achievement ever could.

This chapter invites you to prioritize rest, not just for your body, but for your soul. Find your peace and strength in His loving presence.

✦ Quotes

"Be still and know that I am God."
— Psalm 46:10

"You will find rest for your souls."
— Matthew 11:29

"Sometimes the most productive thing you can do is rest."
— Mark Black

💬 Reflection

Rest is an act of trust. It declares that God is in control, and we do not have to carry everything alone.

When we rest, we realign our hearts to His pace and remember that we are loved for who we are, not just for what we do.

🛕 Prayer

Loving Father,

Thank You for inviting me into Your rest. Help me to slow down, release my burdens, and find renewal in Your presence. Teach me to rest deeply in Your love and care. Amen.

💡 Practical Tips

- Schedule regular quiet time with God.
- Disconnect from devices and distractions to be fully present.
- Practice Sabbath rest weekly.
- Reflect on what restores your soul and make space for it.
- Breathe deeply and meditate on a scripture verse.

🔥 Journaling Prompts

1. What prevents you from resting fully?

_____

_____

_____

_____

_____

2. How do you feel when you rest in God's presence?

_____

_____

_____

_____

3. What changes can you make to prioritize soul rest?

_____

_____

_____

_____

🍃 Affirmation

I find peace and renewal in God's loving presence. I am free to rest.

📖 Scripture

"Come to me, all you who are weary and burdened, and I will give you rest."
— Matthew 11:28

❤️ Reflection Space

CHAPTER 31

CHOOSING FORGIVENESS

Forgiveness is one of the most powerful — and often most difficult — choices we can make. It is not about condoning what was done or forgetting the hurt. It is about freeing ourselves from the weight of bitterness and opening our hearts to healing.

I have struggled with forgiveness, holding on to past offenses to protect myself. But I learned that unforgiveness was a prison, keeping me stuck and robbing me of peace.

This chapter invites you to choose forgiveness — for others, and sometimes, for yourself. It is a gift you give your soul, and it opens the door to true freedom and joy.

✦ Quotes

"Forgive, not because they deserve forgiveness, but because you deserve peace."
— Unknown

"Be kind to one another, tenderhearted, forgiving one another, as God in Christ forgave you."
— Ephesians 4:32

"To forgive is to set a prisoner free and discover that the prisoner was you."
— Lewis B. Smedes

💬 Reflection

Forgiveness is a process, not a one-time event. It may take time and repeated surrender to God. But each step brings more freedom and healing.

Forgiveness does not mean you have to reconcile or allow someone to hurt you again. It simply means you release the hold that anger and pain have over you and trust God to handle justice.

Choose forgiveness today and make space for peace to flourish in your heart.

🛐 Prayer

Merciful God,

Thank You for the forgiveness You freely give me. Help me to extend that same grace to others, even when it is hard. Heal my heart and give me strength to let go of resentment. May Your love be my guide in all things. Amen.

💡 Practical Tips

- Write a letter of forgiveness, even if you never send it.
- Pray for the person you are struggling to forgive.
- Repeat affirmations of release and peace.
- Set boundaries where necessary for your healing.
- Celebrate each small step toward forgiveness.

✍ Journaling Prompts

1. Who do you need to forgive today?

_____

_____

_____

_____

_____

2. How has unforgiveness affected your peace and joy?

_____

_____

_____

_____

_____

3. What would life feel like if you truly let go?

_____

_____

_____

_____

_____

❦ Affirmation

I choose to forgive and free my heart. I walk in God's peace.

📖 Scripture

"Bear with each other and forgive one another if any of you has a grievance against someone. Forgive as the Lord forgave you."

— Colossians 3:13

♥ Reflection Space

CHAPTER 32

STRENGTHENING YOUR FAITH

Faith is like a muscle — it grows stronger when we exercise it. It is easy to believe when life is going smoothly, but true faith is tested and refined in the challenges.

I have walked through valleys where I questioned everything. But in those dark places, I discovered a deeper, stronger faith — one that was not based on feelings, but on God's unchanging promises.

This chapter invites you to strengthen your faith intentionally. Even small, daily acts of trust can build an unshakeable foundation.

✦ Quotes

"Faith does not make things easy; it makes them possible."
— Luke 1:37

"Faith is taking the first step even when you don't see the whole staircase."
— Martin Luther King Jr.

"Let your faith be bigger than your fear."
— Unknown

💬 Reflection

Faith is about trust, not certainty. It means choosing to believe God is promises even when circumstances say otherwise.

When we nurture our faith through prayer, scripture, and community, we become rooted and resilient. We learn to stand firm in storms and to rejoice in the waiting.

🛐 Prayer

Faithful God,

Strengthen my faith each day. Help me to trust You even when I do not understand. Deepen my roots so I can stand firm in every season. Thank You for Your promises that never fail. Amen.

💡 Practical Tips

- Start a daily faith journal recording answered prayers and blessings.
- Memorize and meditate on scriptures about faith.
- Surround yourself with faith-filled people.
- Step out of your comfort zone in small acts of trust.
- Celebrate each moment you choose faith over fear.

⛺ Journaling Prompts

1. Where is God calling you to trust Him more deeply?

_____

_____

_____

_____

_____

2. What fears hold you back from living in full faith?

_____

_____

_____

_____

3. How has God shown His faithfulness in your life?

_____

_____

_____

_____

⚕ Affirmation

My faith grows stronger every day. I trust God completely.

📖 Scripture

"Now faith is confidence in what we hope for and assurance about what we do not see."

— Hebrews 11:1

♥ Reflection Space

CHAPTER 33

LIVING A LIFE OF SERVICE

We live in a world that often focuses on self — self-improvement, self-promotion, self-care. While taking care of ourselves is important, we are also called to serve others. Serving brings us joy, purpose, and connection.

I have found that the most fulfilling moments in my life have been when I poured into someone else's life — a simple act of kindness, a listening ear, a helping hand.

This chapter invites you to live a life of service, using your gifts to make a difference and reflect God's love to the world.

✦ Quotes

"The greatest among you will be your servant."
— Matthew 23:11

"Service to others is the rent you pay for your room here on earth."
— Muhammad Ali

"Small acts, when multiplied by millions of people, can transform the world."
— Howard Zinn

💬 Reflection

Service is not always about grand gestures; it is about being available and present. A smile, a meal, or a word of encouragement can have eternal impact.

When we serve, we step into the heart of Jesus. We become His hands and feet, spreading hope and light wherever we go.

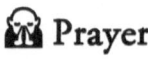 Prayer

Lord,

Thank You for serving me with endless love and grace. Help me to serve others selflessly and joyfully. Open my eyes to opportunities to bless those around me. Use my life to reflect Your kindness and compassion. Amen.

💡 Practical Tips

- Volunteer in your church or community.
- Look for small ways to help someone each day.
- Offer your skills or talents to a friend in need.
- Pray for a heart that is eager to serve.
- Keep a "service journal" to reflect on how you have helped others.

✍ Journaling Prompts

1. Who in your life needs your help right now?

_____

_____

_____

_____

_____

2. What gifts or skills can you use to serve others?

_____

_____

_____

_____

3. How do you feel after you have helped someone?

_____

_____

_____

_____

ϒ Affirmation

I am a servant at heart. I joyfully give and reflect God's love.

📖 Scripture

"Each of you should use whatever gift you have received to serve others."
— 1 Peter 4:10

♥ Reflection Space

CHAPTER 34

COURAGE TO FACE CHALLENGES

Life inevitably brings challenges — unexpected loss, setbacks, fears. But God promises to be with us, to strengthen us, and to give us courage to face whatever comes.

I have learned that courage is not the absence of fear but moving forward despite it. When we rely on God, we find a boldness we never knew we had.

This chapter invites you to face your challenges with courage, knowing you are never alone.

✦ Quotes

"Be strong and courageous. Do not be afraid; do not be discouraged, for the LORD your God will be with you wherever you go."
— Joshua 1:9

"Courage is fear that has said its prayers."
— Dorothy Bernard

"You never know how strong you are until being strong is your only choice."
— Bob Marley

💬 Reflection

Challenges reveal our strength and deepen our faith. Instead of running from them, embrace them as opportunities for growth and transformation.

God equips you for every battle and walks with you every step of the way. Trust that He is your strength and your shield.

🔐 Prayer

Brave Father,

Give me courage to face every challenge with faith and strength. Remind me that You are with me and that Your power is greater than any obstacle I face. Help me to stand firm and move forward boldly. Amen.

💡 Practical Tips

- Repeat empowering scriptures before facing difficult tasks.
- Break big challenges into small, manageable steps.
- Share your struggles with a trusted friend or mentor.
- Celebrate your progress, no matter how small.
- Pray for courage daily.

✍ Journaling Prompts

1. What challenges are you facing right now?

_____

_____

_____

_____

_____

2. What does courage look like to you in this season?

_____

_____

_____

_____

3. How can you rely on God's strength in your challenges?

_____

_____

_____

_____

_____

✨ Affirmation

I am courageous. God's strength empowers me to overcome every challenge.

📖 Scripture

"When I am afraid, I put my trust in you."
— Psalm 56:3

♥ Reflection Space

CHAPTER 35

CELEBRATING YOUR PROGRESS

We often focus so much on where we want to be that we forget to celebrate how far we have come. Every step, every small victory, is worth acknowledging.

Looking back at my journey, I see God's hand in each moment of growth. Each milestone, big or small, is evidence of His faithfulness and our perseverance.

This chapter invites you to pause and celebrate your progress. Gratitude for the journey strengthens your spirit and fuels your future.

✦ Quotes

"Celebrate every win, no matter how small."
— Unknown

"Look how far you've come, not how far you have to go."
— Unknown

"The Lord has done great things for us, and we are filled with joy."
— Psalm 126:3

💬 Reflection

When we celebrate, we honor God's work in our lives. We build confidence and deepen our trust in His plan.

Take time to look back and see the victories — the prayers answered, the mountains climbed, the growth achieved.

Rejoice today and let gratitude fill your heart for all that God has done.

🎧 Prayer

Gracious God,

Thank You for every step of growth and every victory. Help me to pause and celebrate Your faithfulness. Teach me to see progress as a gift and to rejoice in the journey. Amen.

💡 Practical Tips

- Create a "victory jar" to collect moments of progress.
- Share your wins with a friend or loved one.
- Write a gratitude letter to yourself.
- Celebrate milestones with a special treat or small ceremony.
- Reflect on past journal entries to see your growth.

◢ Journaling Prompts

1. What victories can you celebrate today?

_____

_____

_____

_____

_____

2. How has God helped you grow in the past year?

_____

_____

_____

3. What are you most proud of about your journey?

_____

_____

_____

_____

⅄ Affirmation

I celebrate my progress and honor the journey. God has brought me far.

▢ Scripture

"I thank my God every time I remember you."
— Philippians 1:3

♥ Reflection Space

CHAPTER 36

LIVING WITH PURPOSE

Every single one of us was created with a purpose. We are not here by accident — God has a unique plan and calling for each of our lives.

There have been seasons when I felt lost, questioning why I was here and what I was meant to do. But through prayer, reflection, and stepping out in faith, I discovered that purpose is not about big, flashy achievements. It is found in daily acts of love, kindness, and obedience.

This chapter invites you to explore and embrace your God-given purpose. You are here for a reason, and your life has incredible value.

✦ Quotes

"For I know the plans I have for you, declares the LORD, plans to prosper you and not to harm you, plans to give you hope and a future."
— Jeremiah 29:11

"The meaning of life is to find your gift. The purpose of life is to give it away."
— Pablo Picasso

"Your purpose is not the thing you do. It is the thing that happens in others when you do what you do."
— Unknown

💬 Reflection

Living with purpose means aligning your life with God's will. It requires listening to His voice and being willing to step out in faith.

Purpose is found not only in grand gestures but in small, faithful steps. When you serve, love, encourage, and shine your light, you are fulfilling a powerful calling.

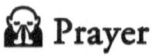 Prayer

Creator God,

Thank You for giving my life purpose. Help me to hear Your voice clearly and to follow the path You have for me. Show me how to use my gifts to bless others and bring glory to You. Amen.

💡 Practical Tips

- Make a list of your gifts and passions.
- Pray daily for God to reveal opportunities to live out your purpose.
- Volunteer in areas that align with your heart.
- Surround yourself with supportive, purpose-driven people.
- Celebrate small moments where you feel aligned with your calling.

✍ Journaling Prompts

1. What do you feel passionate about?

_____

_____

_____

_____

_____

2. How have you seen God use you to impact others?

_____

_____

_____

_____

3. What steps can you take to live more purposefully?

_____

_____

_____

_____

❣ Affirmation

I am created on purpose, for a purpose. I live each day with intention.

📖 Scripture

"We are God's handiwork, created in Christ Jesus to do good works, which God prepared in advance for us to do."

— Ephesians 2:10

💖 Reflection Space

CHAPTER 37

GRATITUDE IN ALL SEASONS

Gratitude is not just for good days; it is a powerful posture that can transform every season of life. Choosing thankfulness in the highs and the lows brings peace and shifts our perspective.

I have learned that gratitude turns what we have into enough. It helps us see God's goodness even in tough times and reminds us that blessings are all around us, waiting to be noticed.

This chapter invites you to cultivate gratitude no matter what season you are in. It is one of the greatest keys to a joyful, peaceful life.

✦ Quotes

"Give thanks in all circumstances; for this is God's will for you in Christ Jesus."
— 1 Thessalonians 5:18

"Gratitude turns what we have into enough."
— Melody Beattie

"A grateful heart sees many blessings."
— Unknown

💬 Reflection

Gratitude does not change our circumstances, but it changes us. It opens our eyes to what God is doing and helps us focus on His goodness.

When we practice gratitude, we find joy even in trivial things and peace even in uncertainty.

🙏 Prayer

Gracious God,

Thank You for every blessing, seen and unseen. Teach me to be grateful in every season, to see Your hand at work in my life. Fill my heart with thankfulness and my lips with praise. Amen.

💡 Practical Tips

- Keep a daily gratitude journal.
- Begin and end each day by listing three things you are thankful for.
- Express your gratitude to others regularly.
- Pause during the day to thank God for small moments.
- Practice speaking blessings aloud instead of complaints.

📓 Journaling Prompts

1. What are you most grateful for today?

_____

_____

_____

_____

_____

_____

2. How has gratitude changed your outlook on life?

_____

_____

_____

_____

_____

_____

3. How can you practice gratitude in challenging seasons?

_____

_____

_____

_____

_____

_____

🍃 Affirmation

I live with a grateful heart. I see blessings in every season.

📖 Scripture

"Enter his gates with thanksgiving and his courts with praise; give thanks to him and praise his name."

— Psalm 100:4

❤ Reflection Space

CHAPTER 38

EMBRACING GOD'S LOVE

God's love is the foundation of everything. It is unconditional, unending, and beyond what we can fully understand. When we truly embrace His love, it transforms how we see ourselves and how we live.

For years, I struggled to accept God's love fully, feeling unworthy or thinking I needed to earn it. But His love is a gift — freely given and always available.

This chapter invites you to open your heart and receive God's love deeply and completely. Let it be the anchor of your life.

✦ Quotes

"I have loved you with an everlasting love."
— Jeremiah 31:3

"God loves each of us as if there were only one of us."
— Augustine

"Nothing can separate us from God's love."
— Romans 8:39

💬 Reflection

God's love is not based on your performance but on His nature. You are loved right now, just as you are.

Embracing this love brings healing, freedom, and joy. Let it sink deep into your heart and overflow into every area of your life.

🛕 Prayer

Heavenly Father,

Thank You for loving me unconditionally. Help me to receive and believe in Your love fully. Let it transform my heart and guide my actions each day. Amen.

💡 Practical Tips

- Read and meditate on scriptures about God's love daily.
- Write affirmations that remind you of His love.
- Practice self-compassion and kindness to yourself.
- Surround yourself with reminders of His love (art, music, books).
- Share God's love with others through acts of kindness.

✍ Journaling Prompts

1. What does God's love mean to you personally?

_____

_____

_____

_____

_____

2. What keeps you from fully accepting His love?

_____

_____

_____

_____

3. How can you remind yourself of His love daily?

_____

_____

_____

_____

⸙ Affirmation

God deeply loves me. His love defines and sustains me.

📖 Scripture

"See what great love the Father has lavished on us, that we should be called children of God!"

— 1 John 3:1

❤ Reflection Space

CHAPTER 39

BECOMING MORE LIKE CHRIST

The Christian journey is not just about belief — it is about transformation. God's desire is for us to become more like His Son, Jesus.

Becoming more like Christ means reflecting His character: love, kindness, humility, patience, and compassion. It is a daily process of growth and surrender.

This chapter invites you to embrace the lifelong journey of transformation, becoming more like Jesus in every area of your life.

 Quotes

"Follow God's example, therefore, as dearly loved children."
— Ephesians 5:1

"Christlikeness is your eventual destination, but your journey will last a lifetime."
— Rick Warren

"The goal of the Christian life is not just to get us into heaven but to get heaven into us."
— Unknown

💬 Reflection

Becoming like Christ is not about perfection but progression. It is about allowing His Spirit to shape us day by day.

As we spend time with Him, we begin to think, speak, and act more like Him. This transformation brings peace, purpose, and deep joy.

🛐 Prayer

Lord Jesus,

help me to become more like You every day. Transform my heart and mind. Teach me to love as You love, to serve as You serve, and to walk in humility and grace. Amen.

💡 Practical Tips

- Spend daily time in God's Word and prayer.
- Reflect on Christ's character and how you can embody it.
- Ask for feedback from trusted friends on areas to grow.
- Practice intentional acts of love and kindness.
- Surrender daily habits and thoughts that do not align with Christ.

✍ Journaling Prompts

1. In what ways do you want to become more like Christ?

_____

_____

_____

_____

2. What areas of your life need His transformation most?

_____

_____

_____

_____

3. How can you reflect His love to others today?

_____

_____

_____

_____

❣ Affirmation

I am being transformed daily to be more like Christ. His love shines through me.

📖 Scripture

"And we all, who with unveiled faces contemplate the Lord's glory, are being transformed into his image with ever-increasing glory."

— 2 Corinthians 3:18

♥ Reflection Space

CHAPTER 40

LIVING EACH DAY WITH HOPE

Hope is the anchor of our souls. It keeps us steady when the storms of life come and reminds us that God's promises are true.

There have been times when I felt hopeless when the future looked uncertain and dark. But even in those moments, God whispered hope into my heart, reminding me that He is always working for my good.

This concluding chapter invites you to live each day with hope — a hope that does not disappoint because it is rooted in God's unchanging love and faithfulness.

✦ Quotes

"May the God of hope fill you with all joy and peace as you trust in him."
— Romans 15:13

"Hope is being able to see that there is light despite all of the darkness."
— Desmond Tutu

"With God, all things are possible."
— Matthew 19:26

💬 Reflection

Hope is not dreaming; it is confident expectation in God's promises. It gives us strength to keep going, joy to keep smiling, and faith to keep believing.

No matter what you face, hold on to hope. God has a beautiful future for you, and He is faithful to fulfill His word.

🛕 Prayer

God of Hope,

Fill me with Your hope today and every day. Help me to trust in Your promises and to look forward with joyful expectation. Strengthen my faith and remind me that with You, all things are possible. Amen.

💡 Practical Tips

- Write down God's promises and read them daily.
- Surround yourself with hopeful, faith-filled people.
- Speak words of hope and encouragement to yourself and others.
- Visualize and pray over your hopes for the future.
- Celebrate small signs of God's goodness today.

✍ Journaling Prompts

1. What are you hoping for in this season?

_____
_____
_____
_____
_____

2. How has God given you hope in the past?

_____
_____
_____
_____
_____

3. What promises of God give you strength today?

_____
_____
_____
_____
_____

⅌ Affirmation

I live each day anchored in God's hope. My future is bright in Him.

📖 Scripture

"Let us hold unswervingly to the hope we profess, for he who promised is faithful."
— Hebrews 10:23

❤️ Reflection Space

CHAPTER 41

WALKING BOLDLY INTO YOUR FUTURE

As we come to the end of this book, it is truly just the beginning of your next chapter. You have spent time reflecting, praying, journaling, and growing now it is time to take those seeds planted in your heart and watch them bloom as you move forward boldly.

God has incredible plans for you — plans far greater than you can imagine. He calls you to walk forward with confidence and assurance, not held back by fear, past failures, or lingering doubts. Every setback you have experienced, every tear you have shed, and every prayer you have whispered has been part of shaping you into the strong, resilient person you are today. You are not defined by your past, but by the promises God has spoken over your life.

Stepping into your future requires courage. It means choosing faith even when the path is not clear and trusting God's timing even when you feel impatient or uncertain. It means believing that you are worthy of His blessings and capable of carrying out the purpose He has placed within you. Remember, He is already in your tomorrow, preparing the way ahead. He is arranging divine connections, opening doors you cannot yet see, and equipping you for every challenge and triumph to come.

This chapter is an invitation — a holy summons — to take all the lessons, prayers, and affirmations you have gathered here and carry them into your daily life with boldness and joy. You are not stepping forward alone. God goes before you, making crooked places straight, and He walks beside you as a faithful companion and guide. You have His promise that He will never leave you nor forsake you.

When you face moments of fear, remind yourself of the victories He has already given you. When doubt whispers in your ear, speak His truth louder. When you feel weak, remember that His strength is made perfect in your weakness. You were created to do hard things, to love deeply, to shine brightly, and to leave a legacy of faith.

Today, decide to walk boldly into your future. Embrace the unknown with open hands and an open heart, trusting that God's goodness and mercy will follow you all the days of your life. Live each day with expectancy, knowing that the best is yet to come.

Reflection Questions:

- What fears or doubts do you need to release as you step forward?
- What dreams or goals has God placed on your heart for this next season?
- How can you practically apply the lessons from this book to your daily life?

Prayer:

Lord, thank You for the journey I have walked through these pages. Thank You for the growth, the healing, and the revelation You have given me. I ask for Your courage as I step into my future. Help me to trust You completely, to walk in faith and not by sight. Strengthen me to let go of the past and embrace the beautiful future You have prepared for me. I declare that I will walk boldly, knowing that You go before me and Your plans for me are good. In Jesus' name, amen.

✦ Quotes

"For we walk by faith, not by sight."
— 2 Corinthians 5:7

"The best way to predict your future is to create it with God."
— Unknown

"God has already been where you are going. Trust His plan."
— Unknown

💬 Reflection

It is easy to feel afraid when stepping into something new — a new season, a new dream, a new challenge. But when we focus on God's faithfulness rather than our fears, boldness rises within us.

Walking boldly is not about having it all figured out. It is about knowing who goes with you and who has gone before you. You do not need all the answers today; you just need faith for the next step.

Trust that God has equipped you with everything you need. Move forward knowing you are deeply loved and fully supported by His grace.

💡 Practical Tips

- Write down a vision statement for your future and pray over it.
- Set small, faith-based action steps toward your goals.
- Surround yourself with people who encourage your growth and support your journey.
- Revisit your journal and affirmations often to stay inspired.
- Celebrate every step forward, no matter how small.

🔖 Journaling Prompts

1. What dreams or goals is God placing on your heart right now?

_____

_____

_____

_____

_____

2. What fears might be holding you back, and how can you surrender them to God?

_____

_____

_____

_____

3. What steps can you take today to move forward boldly?

_____

_____

_____

_____

🌱 Affirmation

I walk boldly into my future, knowing God is with me and His plans for me are good.

📖 Scripture

"'For I know the plans I have for you,' declares the LORD, 'plans to prosper you and not to harm you, plans to give you hope and a future.'"

— Jeremiah 29:11

❤ Reflection Space

 ACKNOWLEDGMENTS

First and foremost, I thank God the Author of life, the Giver of every good gift, and the One who fills my heart with faith and my mouth with words. Without His love, grace, and endless mercy, this book and every chapter of my life would not be possible. To Him be all the glory.

To my incredible parents: thank you for your endless love, sacrifices, and prayers. You taught me the importance of faith, integrity, and perseverance. Your unwavering belief in me laid the foundation for every dream I have dared to chase.

To my amazing siblings: thank you for your laughter, your encouragement, and the special bond we share. You have been my first friends and lifelong cheerleaders, always reminding me to stay true to who I am.

To my extended family: your support has been a constant source of strength. Thank you for standing with me through every season and for always reminding me where I come from.

To my pastor and spiritual leaders: thank you for pouring into me with wisdom, guidance, and prayer. Your leadership and example have helped shape my walk with God and inspired me to grow deeper in my faith.

To my dear friends: thank you for the late-night talks, the words of encouragement, and the way you show up in both the good times and the hard ones. Your love has been a beautiful reminder of God's grace in human form.

To my mentor: your guidance, honesty, and belief in me have been instrumental on this journey. Thank you for challenging me to dream bigger, pray harder, and never settle for less than God's best.

To every reader who picks up this book: thank you for inviting me into your mornings, your quiet reflections, and your spiritual journey. It is an honor to share these words with you. May they encourage your heart, strengthen your faith, and remind you that you are deeply loved.

And finally, to everyone who believed in this dream and pushed me to see it through this book is for you. Thank you, sincerely, for every prayer, every word of support, and every moment you chose to believe in me.

With all my love and gratitude.
Calvin Allen

ISBN: 979-8-218-74489-2